Great Traits

Great Traits

Investigating the behaviour
and beliefs behind phenomenal feats

TOBIAS HARWOOD

PHOTOGRAPHY BY NICO WILLS

GREATTRAITSPROJECT

Inspired by one wounded soldier.
Dedicated to all wounded soldiers.

All royalties from this book are donated to the charity
Walking With The Wounded.

Walking With The Wounded was inspired by extraordinary people, men and women who overcame their injuries, reflected in the remarkable stories within *Great Traits*. Time and again we see individuals achieving goals which too often are labelled as impossible, proving that with courage, determination and mental strength nearly everything is possible. The charity is privileged and honoured to be benefitting from the sale of this book where Tobias Harwood perfectly captures the nature of greatness within people who are humble and selfless, and without this fascinating exploration of human nature none of us would be able to appreciate. The proceeds will be able to provide further support to the beneficiaries of Walking With The Wounded, those who are physically, mentally and socially disadvantaged post their service. While the majority transition out of the Armed Forces and find a sustainable and secure future in the civilian world, some find it challenging, and they find themselves homeless or in the criminal justice system, with many suffering from mental ill health. So often these people are ignored, but we believe they are as deserving as anyone else who has served. These are the people we support and by buying this book, you are helping us make a difference to these men and women – thank you.

Edward Parker
Founder & CEO
Walking With The Wounded

Contents

Introduction

Afghanistan, 4 July 2009

In the oppressive heat of an Afghan summer, Operation Panther Claw is underway. It's the first significant push by British troops to control the rising insurgency in these lawless and hostile lands. For the soldiers leading the attack, the stifling heat is exacerbated by a layer of thick body armour and the claustrophobic interior of their small armoured vehicle.

The patrol advance in single file across the arid landscape. The heavy air leaves a thin blanket of dust in every crevice of the soldiers' uniforms. An eerie quietness belies the risk that surrounds them. Suddenly, the silence is broken by the whistle of compressing air, followed by a devastating explosion as a rocket propelled grenade hits its mark. The Light Dragoons infantry regiment is under attack.

The RPG pierces the side of the armoured Spartan vehicle, immediately concussing all of the trapped soldiers. Violent reverberations perforate their eardrums leaving behind a piercing ringing inside their skulls. Amongst the horror and tumult, confusion reigns. Molten metal rips through the shell of the armoured vehicle, showing no mercy. Private Robbie Laws is killed instantly. Meanwhile, Captain Guy Disney is lucky to be alive: the explosion has torn through his right leg and the stench of burning flesh is overwhelming. Within minutes, he is evacuated on a helicopter back to Camp Bastion for triage. He has escaped death, but at a price: his injuries leave the surgeons with no choice but to amputate the remainder of his leg.

1

For Guy, rehabilitation awaits, and the start of a different – and difficult – chapter in his life.

Guy isn't the only British soldier to have been injured during the war in Afghanistan – between 2006 and 2013 over two thousand wounded troops were admitted to field hospitals while 455 British personnel lost their lives. However, Guy's injuries, though far from unique, had a greater resonance for me, given how long I had known him and our close friendship.

Growing up, Guy and I were thick as thieves. We attended the same school in Malvern and lived only a few miles apart in the Cotswolds. We were partners in crime, with a reputation for mischief and unrelenting pranks. Our favourite pastime involved collecting water balloons or French bangers and attacking each other in the back garden. As soon as we hit puberty, we graduated from collecting fireworks to frantically pursuing the opposite sex, with mixed success. We also made a habit of frequenting the various country pubs between our two villages in order to discuss the finest betting tips for next week's horse racing. After several drinks, the debate would often stretch to whether we were going to end up too heavy to make it as professional jockeys ourselves.

Like our sense of humour, our interests and academic abilities were similar. We were deeply mediocre students resigned to extra mathematics and English lessons thanks to another shared attribute: dyslexia. From an early age, Guy was far more interested in how to construct a shelter or light a fire than in academia. My dyslexia, meanwhile, was so debilitating that for many years I struggled to differentiate between the letter 'b' and the letter 'd' – an embarrassing nuisance when regularly misspelling my own name, Toby.

After finishing school and university, Guy and I accepted the reality that careers as jockeys were unlikely to be forthcoming. Instead, we opted for more conventional career paths: I chose a suit and went into the City while Guy donned a uniform and joined the army. In fact, within our circle of friends, I suspect we were regarded as two amiable lads with a healthy appetite for laughter and not much else.

The attack in July 2009 changed all that. From the moment the RPG hit Guy's armoured vehicle it was clear that his life would change. He endured countless operations to heal his amputated limb and then began the slow process of learning to walk again with the aid of a prosthetic leg. Guy faced many days, weeks and months of rehabilitation that would ultimately alter how he interacted with the world around him. Yet, it was not the physical changes of an amputee that I noticed most in my close friend. The profound change in Guy wasn't the prosthetic attached to his leg – it was his frame of mind.

In the immediate aftermath of the amputation, Guy still possessed the same superb sense of humour. I remember talking to him in Headley Court – the Ministry of Defence's rehabilitation centre in Surrey – and his relentless wisecracking was as prominent as ever, but I soon sensed a new level of determination to him. There was an unprecedented clarity to his thoughts as well as a level of grit and a sense of purpose that I found inspiring. It was a mindset that, until that point, had been dormant. While I had often regarded his jokes as outstanding, he had excelled at little else. As Guy's recovery took shape, my perception of him began to alter.

Against all logic, Guy had suddenly begun to excel. By early 2011, just eighteen months after his right leg amputation, Guy became the first amputee to ever reach the North Pole. Soon after, he went on to become one of the first amputees to reach the South Pole. To this day, he remains the only amputee who has completed both Polar journeys.

Beyond simply being a friend and an exemplary jester, Guy has become a great source of inspiration to me. I was fascinated by his mental transformation and I became curious as to how my previously happy-go-lucky friend had found this new drive, determination and discipline to accomplish such astonishing feats. What was his psychology? What was driving him to such remarkable achievements?

The change I had witnessed was so extraordinary that my curiosity began to spread. Did other Britons, who had also achieved remarkable feats, benefit from a similar state of mind? I began to investigate if there were similarities in their character traits, thought processes and beliefs. Was there anything that could be learned from their attitudes? If so, I began to speculate that, perhaps, anyone could go on to improve their own lives by assimilating such lessons.

In short, my friend Guy and the mindset behind his remarkable achievements led me to delve deeper and write this book.

* * *

It was a typical drizzly English morning when I met Guy at his Cotswold stone cottage in the village of Laverton to interview him. Despite the persistent rain, Guy, as hospitable as ever, walked down the garden path to greet me. As I shook his hand, I felt apprehensive. As well as I knew Guy, it was unheard of for us to sit down and have a serious discussion. For a man once described by an ex-girlfriend as 'emotionally numb', I knew that getting answers to difficult questions may prove problematic, or at least, he would evade answering using his trademark humour. As it turned out, I needn't have worried. As Guy put the kettle on, I settled down at his kitchen table with his faithful black Labrador, Twiga, at my side. Five hours later our conversation subsided and I had teased out some fascinating insights.

We started talking about the first few weeks after the attack. "My goal was to go back to Afghanistan," he said. "I hated the idea of my blokes being out in Afghan while I was at Headley Court. I was racked with guilt. I was determined to return to Afghanistan and get out of hospital as quickly as possible and I thought that the best way to get better was to set goals and challenge myself. I wanted to beat the recovery time of what any other amputee had achieved. Normally people spend about six months there but I was out in about a month and a half."

By late August 2009 – just six weeks after the amputation – Guy was up on his prosthetic and shuffling around. He was so determined to complete his recovery that he began targeting a return to Afghanistan with the Light Dragoons in October that same year. "I wanted to go back to Afghan," he continued. "So I had to pass the fitness tests. I started training for them but my stump burst open, it was very bloody. I remember feeling physically exhausted and the reality of the situation became clear. There was no way I could have gone back so quickly. Looking back, my aim was ludicrous. I was still very sick. I still had a very raw wound."

Guy failed the fitness tests, but his drive was undimmed. He recovered and returned to duty in record time. "I was determined to get out of Headley Court as quickly as possible and by January 2010 I was well recovered and back at work," he recalled. Around this time, Guy received an interesting e-mail: the charity Walking With The Wounded were searching for volunteers to complete what would be a world first for an amputee – an expedition to the Geographic North Pole. "As soon as I read it I immediately knew I wanted to go," Guy explained. "I had been looking for a challenge and going back to Afghanistan was very high on my list. But I also I wanted to do something that would be arduous irrespective of being injured."

Guy met the expedition organisers and Walking With The Wounded founders Edward Parker and Simon Daglish. "All kinds of different soldiers turned up," Guy remembered. "Some missing one leg, some missing both legs or an arm and some soldiers with colostomy bags. Ed and Simon were looking for soldiers who were two years post-injury as they thought that was sufficient time for an injury to stabilise enough." Feeling slighted, it was a condition that made Guy even more determined to take part.

Guy decided to set his own training regime to prove he was ready. He replicated the strain of pulling a sledge by dragging old car tyres four times a week and, gradually, he built up to a distance of ten miles a day to harden his stump and establish his fitness for the expedition. Three months later, when the shortlisted group of expedition candidates travelled to Spitsbergen for acclimatisation and training, Guy proved his competence and was selected.

I asked Guy about the attitude that had driven him. "I am competitive," he replied. "I will always look at what someone else has achieved and try to beat it. When I arrived at Selly Oak Hospital I was told six weeks was the norm for a below-the-knee amputee to recover. I immediately thought – I want to be out of here quicker than that. There were lots of people there with amputations and I wanted to leave before them, because then I would win that little battle.

"After that, I wanted to return to Afghan because very few amputees had ever managed to go back. Then I wanted to do the North Pole because I thought it would be hard and nobody had done it. I do it for myself and not so others can pat me on the back. *Can't, won't and shouldn't* are the most motivating words out there. When someone tells me I can't do something I immediately want to prove them wrong."

The North Pole expedition set off on 29 March 2011. The target was as simple as it was hard: to cover three hundred miles of frozen Arctic Ocean completely unaided and reach the Geographic North Pole in approximately twenty-five days. The daily target was thirteen miles per day, across terrain riddled with ice rubble and pressure ridges which would push their resilience to the limit.

The challenge of covering three hundred miles was exacerbated by the Arctic's unique challenges. Unlike continental Antarctica, the ice of the Arctic is never a certainty and it constantly drifts, leaving any expeditions at the mercy of currents. The shifting ice also creates large fractures between the sea ice and carrying a 100kg sledge while negotiating these fissures carries the risk of hypothermia or a swift death if submerged in the icy waters for even a short while. The ambient temperature in the Arctic readily falls to –40°C, with regular cloud cover diminishing any warmth offered by the sun's rays, while there is always the added risk of encountering a famished polar bear.

Guy told me about the conditions he faced on the expedition: "In the tent, you are in your sleeping bag, where your body is warm, except your nose and cheeks that are exposed to the freezing air. You wake up with a cold face and a freezing nose. If you put your nose inside the sleeping bag the moisture then freezes and you wake up to a layer of frost inside your sleeping bag. It's not very comfy. You wake up in the morning and, even though it is –40°C, you have to prise yourself out of your sleeping bag and put it outside the tent because it's completely flammable and you can't light the burner with the sleeping bag in the tent. To light the cooker requires a pump and a bottle, but if you touch the bottle with bare skin you will get stuck to it and the ice will burn your skin, so you have to use foam to hold it. You are doing all this while you are physically shaking in –40°C. Furthermore, all the moisture you breathe freezes on the inside of the tent so if you accidentally knock the side you get a snow shower. Once you get the cooker going, you huddle around it to feel some warmth. Then in the morning you spend two hours melting your snow for food and water for the day."

If that wasn't enough, Guy faced further challenges because of his prosthetic leg. "I found the hard part was putting my leg on in the morning, because it was sore," he said. "When you are doing thirteen miles a day on a stump, you are bound to get blisters and be sore but I then had to attach the prosthetic on top of that and it was freezing cold. I have also got shrapnel in my leg and the shrapnel comes to the surface in extreme heat or extreme cold, so each morning I was putting something freezing cold on to a leg that was blistered and had the odd bit of metal coming off. I definitely started to dread the mornings."

I asked Guy how he dealt with this and he explained, "I started playing mind games with myself. I would treat the leg as a different part of me. For the first half an hour every day, it physically hurt. I was skiing along and I realised, I have half an hour of this but actually this is one of the only things I have got to think about. There is not much else to focus on. Quite often your iPod would freeze solid, so you wouldn't be able to listen to any audio books or music. So I recognised that it broke up my day and I would deliberately use it as something to think about. For the rest of the day the leg would niggle a bit, mainly when we stopped to eat (every two hours for ten minutes). I would actually take pleasure from it; when somebody came up to me and asked how I was feeling I would reply, 'I'm fine'. I treated it like a game and tried to hide it. If they didn't know I was injured it was as though I had won. That became my little game each day. Ultimately, I wanted to go to the North Pole. How much did I want to go to the North Pole? More than the pain in my leg. Done."

I found Guy's attitude to dealing with pain instructive: "I am a strong believer that if you have a problem there is no point mentioning it and bringing someone else into the circle as it only spoils their day. If you have got a headache and there is no paracetamol then why mention it? It is selfish to bring the other person into that negative spiral. If I was having a really tough time I would just look at someone who was having a worse time than me and realise they were still going. You could always tell when someone was suffering because they would be further behind than you and would be skiing slower. I always thought that if they were still going that meant I certainly could keep going. You take one step and then you do another step and, suddenly, you are half a foot further on than you were."

Using a colourful metaphor to illustrate his point Guy said, "Reaching the North Pole is a bit like eating an elephant: you don't do it all in one go. You can only do it slowly and piece by piece. But, eventually, you can eat the whole lot. You also reflect on how lucky you are to be doing the expedition – there are a lot of people who couldn't take part in the expedition because they were too badly injured or they were no longer alive."

The expedition posed relentless challenge and with little respite from the elements. Pressure ridges – like tectonic plates pushed together to form ice rubble – were a particular challenge. These randomly formed angular ice blocks range from a few inches to a few metres in height. In some cases a field of pressure ridges continued for a few kilometres and dramatically slowed the progress of the expedition.

"The only positive was that the pressure ridges made it interesting and helped break up your day," Guy explained. The physical exertion of hauling a heavy sledge over the jagged obstacles added the risk of overheating and the challenge of controlling the body's core temperature. "The moment you feel warm it means you are going to start sweating. As soon as you start sweating the sweat freezes up and all your clothing becomes ineffective. So you must remain slightly uncomfortable and never comfortable." Having completed each day's target one final daily challenge always confronted Guy. "To end the day you pitch your tent and melt snow for three hours to rehydrate and cook supper," he said. "You climb into your sleeping bag as quickly as possible and got some sleep, albeit a restless sleep. It all repeats itself again the next day."

Throughout the description of his remarkable journey I was struck by Guy's deeply constructive mindset. His relentlessly objective outlook ensures the amputation does not limit him in any respect. Indeed, he doesn't even fully acknowledge the presence of an injury. "The injury, in my mind, has been and gone," he continued. "I am over it. I have adapted. There is no injury. There could be a blister on my stump but that's not because my leg has been blown off. I could just as easily have a blister on my other foot. I did the London Marathon this year and completed it slowly in four hours and nineteen minutes and people congratulated me. But they are only saying that because I am missing a leg. What time should I be doing if I wasn't missing a leg? I think under three hours and thirty minutes is a good marathon time so, for my own benefit, I would like to do a marathon under three hours thirty minutes."

I asked him about the effect the Arctic expedition had had on him. "The North Pole did me a lot of good because I think I hadn't been tested post injury and I needed a test. I got personal satisfaction from the North Pole. Interestingly, I didn't from the South Pole because I didn't feel challenged in the Antarctic, which sounds arrogant but I genuinely wasn't tested. I was in my comfort zone. Once you show you are capable of doing something it no longer seems like such a big achievement. In Afghan, you are tested and it puts you up against it but in the best kind of way. Many of us who went out to Afghan will not talk about it but, for me, getting shot at and shooting back gives you the feeling that you have got to be sharp. The adrenaline rush of being shot at is something you can never replicate."

As our kitchen table conversation drew to a close it was clear to me that Guy possessed a number of key character traits that underlined his remarkable achievements: he displayed an extraordinary level of grit and determination, he was intrinsically motivated, he actively sought to push himself beyond his comfort zone and he adopted a constructive interpretation of the adversity he experienced.

My initial interview with Guy inspired me to investigate further. Over the next three years I interviewed an array of *Great Britons* from deliberately diverse domains; from sports stars to explorers, business leaders to ballerinas and scientists to musicians. I crafted a consistent set of questions for all the interviewees and analysed their responses. What I found was a remarkable consistency in terms of character and mindset and, more specifically, I identified five definitive traits that drive the interviewees to achieve phenomenal feats.

This book distils the behaviour and beliefs behind the Britons' phenomenal feats. These are remarkable individuals with an array of wonderful stories to tell but, beyond that, it is an insight into a worldview that can both inspire and influence us all in our own lives. In the chapters that follow I will introduce you to these amazing individuals who I have been privileged to meet – some are household names while others are unsung heroes, all have an attitude to life we can learn from.

The definition of what constitutes a 'phenomenal feat' is, of course, subjective. Recognising the remarkable achievements of an individual can be clearly quantifiable in some instances; winning an Olympic gold medal or becoming World Champion, for example. In other areas – like devoting your life's work to charity or starting your own company from scratch – what constitutes greatness is less clear cut and, for the purposes of this book, is at the qualitative discretion of the author. The aim is not to investigate what constitutes a great Briton, per se, but to discover how these particular Britons think.

The following pages will reveal the crucial character traits that drive these particular Britons to achieve remarkable feats. What emerged consistently from my interviews is not a singular secret to success but, rather, five specific traits.

The five sections that follow reveal the five *Great Traits*. Each section begins and concludes with a case study, highlighting an interviewee who typifies that particular character trait in abundance.

In section one we outline the first trait; *passion*. The importance of intrinsic motivation is paramount, it leads to focus and is a precursor to *grit* and persistence, which are investigated in section two. In section three we see the role of *competitiveness*, while section four highlights the importance of *boldness* and pushing yourself beyond your comfort zone and how this fuels self-belief.

The last and most encompassing trait is the importance of a *constructive consciousness*. All prior traits are encased in the *Great Britons'* relentlessly constructive attitude and the fascinating insight that they believe you are always able to choose your own mindset.

"Be not afraid of greatness," Shakespeare wrote in *Twelfth Night*. "Some are born great, some achieve greatness and others have greatness thrust upon them." Over the following pages, we will discover individuals from each of the categories. I found them hugely inspiring and their insights truly enriching. I hope that you do too.

Trait 1
PASSION

Chapter 1

Case Study: Levison Wood

"At the age of eighteen, I went off travelling and I got the bug. For me travelling became not just a passion but the way I wanted to live my life."

Levison Wood is an explorer, best-selling author and photographer. His *passion* for adventure has driven him to the most remote and inhospitable corners of the earth. In 2014, he completed a remarkable nine-month expedition walking the entire length of the River Nile, which was documented in a critically acclaimed Channel 4 series. In 2015, he embarked on an even more ambitious challenge to walk the length of the Himalayas from Afghanistan to Bhutan. He has recorded stories and expeditions from around the world for a decade and his work has been featured on the BBC, National Geographic, Discovery Channel and CNN.

From an early age, it was clear that Levison's *passion* for adventure was not going to be satiated by his small village upbringing in Staffordshire. "I went to a comprehensive school where there were no notable alumni," he recalls. "As a seven-year-old I remember thinking that I didn't want to do something normal with my life. I loved the stories and biographies of Lawrence of Arabia, David Livingstone and Captain Scott and that inspired me to be an adventurer. I wanted to go and command soldiers in battle. I wanted to go and see places that nobody had ever heard of."

These vivid imprints in Lev's mind served as a constant propeller behind his epic journeys. "It was the long overland expeditions that really inspired me to want to do it full time," he says. "I developed an interest in photography and, particularly, writing; it was always my ambition to become a writer but to do that I needed to have enough stories to tell. So I decided to do something useful and practical first and I joined the army. I went to Sandhurst and served as an Officer in the Parachute Regiment."

During his army career, Lev completed multiple tours of Afghanistan fighting against Taliban insurgents in the provinces of Helmand, Kandahar and Zabul but it was his *passion* for travel and writing that led him to set up his own business. "I set up an expedition company using the skills that I'd learnt in the army to take people to remote places," he recounts. "It took about three years to set up the company after I had left the army and, during that time, I couldn't afford to pay rent so I had to sleep on friends' floors and sacrifices had to be made." Lev and his company went on to lead walking expeditions across Madagascar, Iraq, Afghanistan and other treacherous post-conflict zones.

Despite the lack of obvious financial rewards, Lev persisted in pursuing his *passion* for writing and travelling. "I became a full-time photographer and writer and I was writing for guidebooks, newspapers and magazines, but I realised it didn't pay very well and, ultimately, I wanted to write a book. I knew that I needed to do one big expedition to get the ball rolling, so I decided to walk the length of the Nile. It took over two years of planning, pitching, fundraising, and organising. I managed to convince Channel 4 to commission the story of my journey as a series and the book deal emerged off the back of that."

The audacious challenge of walking the River Nile took seven million steps and nine months to complete. The 4,250 mile journey started in the highlands of Rwanda and followed the river on its meandering course through the jungles of Tanzania and Uganda, around Lake Victoria and into South Sudan. After navigating the immense wetlands of the Sudd swamp, Lev crossed into North Sudan, traversed the Sahara Desert and Lake Nasser and then entered Egypt for a final 1,000 mile walk to the Mediterranean Sea.

Armed with just a backpack and his survival skills he faced an arduous physical and mental test through Africa's most remote and hostile locations. Lev encountered mercenaries, poachers and missionaries and came face to face with hippos, crocodiles and lions. He crossed the Sahara and visited countries forged out of the ruins of war and revolution. Much like his boyhood inspiration, he visited the Great Lakes and the exact location where legendary explorer David Livingstone met reporter Henry Stanley by Lake Tanganyika. Lev retraced the Arab slave routes and slept in Bedouin tents before his eventual arrival at the Mediterranean shore.

In a resolute adherence to his childhood dream, Levison is determined to explore the most remote locations and avoid conforming to a career of normality. "It's the weirdest thing: I don't feel comfortable in my comfort zone," he admits. "If I'm comfortable, then I feel as though I have to move on. Having itchy feet has its drawbacks because it means you're constantly wanting new challenges and experiences to make yourself feel like you're achieving something."

For Levison, his *passion* for writing and adventure never falls into the category of drudgery. "It doesn't feel like work at all. I feel as though I gave up work when I left the army," he says with laughter. "The army wasn't really work either, to be honest. I can't say I've ever had a proper job. I think when you do something you enjoy you don't see it as work; I certainly don't. I'm following my dream that I've had since as long as I can remember."

Following the success of the Nile expedition Levison set his sights on an even greater challenge, to walk the length of the world's highest mountain range. The Himalayas, known as the 'roof of the world', are a hostile environment that few outsiders ever dare to see. The grueling 1,700 miles took four million steps starting from Afghanistan and ending in Bhutan four-months later. The challenges he faced included snow, ice, altitude sickness and treacherous earthquake-devastated landscapes. Navigating the isolated Afghan valleys and the Line of Control between Pakistan and Indian Kashmir were equally intimidating and perilous.

Levison's expedition was interrupted halfway by an horrific car crash in Nepal. After arriving in a Nepalese village, Lev and his travelling companion Binod Pariyar were moved on by the communist leaders who had taken control in a local coup. They were forced into a car late at night and while travelling back down a narrow mountain road, the brakes failed and the vehicle flew over the edge of a five hundred foot cliff and into a jungle ravine. The car rolled a dozen times, treating the passengers like rag dolls, and shattered Lev's arm in the process. "I could quite easily be dead now," Lev reflects. "I'm very grateful to be alive." With minimal medical facilities in the remote Nepalese village nearby, he was flown back to the UK for surgery, had plates installed in his arm and now has a twelve-inch scar as a constant reminder of that night in Nepal. Despite this catastrophic setback and against medical advice recommending otherwise, Levison was back in the Himalayas five weeks later to continue the expedition.

For Levison, such perils are part of the appeal and only serve to fuel his enthusiasm for his chosen path. "If you're walking for months there can be times when not much changes so you, in fact, want something to happen," he says. "Yes, there were terrifying moments, like being chased by an elephant, but it's exciting when it happens. It's a bit like when you are in the army and you go to Afghanistan; of course you don't want to get shot at but you do relish the excitement and the adrenaline if it happens because it's what you've trained to do."

Overall, Levison's love for adventure spurs him on to treacherous locations and to achieve spectacular feats of physical and mental endurance. His *passion* propels him towards the most remote locations on earth where he can record his experiences via his love for writing and photography. "I don't think I ever lost the belief in my dream," he says. "I don't know if that's because I was a self-deluded child or because I never grew up but, either way, I stuck to my guns and followed it through. What motivated me was having a childhood dream and not giving in or settling."

Chapter 2

Pursuing your Passion

Is it possible to truly define what *passion* is? When seen through the prism of a selection of remarkable Britons, the term becomes less ambiguous and something that vividly connects the individuals in this book. In short, it becomes something distillable.

Passion is the deep-rooted motivation which the inspirational people in this book espoused countless times when interviewed. As Guy Disney stresses: "I do it for myself and not so others can pat me on the back." For Levison Wood, adventure and travel writing were such ardent passions that they became the focus of his life.

The word *passion* embodies the ceaseless desire to pursue a chosen path, despite external uncertainties. It represents the combination of devotion and decisiveness when doubters may be counselling otherwise. As Guy bluntly puts it: "*Can't, won't and shouldn't* are the most motivating words out there."

Even when the challenges seem difficult or insurmountable, such as walking to the North Pole with a prosthetic leg, or walking 4,000 miles along the River Nile, there is a sense of conviction and a motivation that propels these remarkable individuals forward.

For these individuals, relentlessly pursuing their chosen path results in positive externalities. Intense intrinsic motivation leads to remarkable levels of commitment, devotion and enthusiasm – the external manifestation of an individual's drive. So extreme can the devotion be that families and friendships are often eschewed. There is a deep sense of vocation amongst them – the sense of belief and enthusiasm for what they do is almost religious in its fervour.

Not only do these individuals love what they do but their enthusiasm is infectious and they are eager to encourage others to pursue their respective dreams. Noticeably, there is little differentiation between work and play for them, augmented by a unique ability to sustain hours of intense focus and concentration. Hours of practise are no longer a burden but an opportunity to learn and refine one's chosen path. Any obstacle or setback is not a disincentive but serves as an opportunity to improve and develop.

Overall, the combination of intrinsic motivation with the commitment, devotion and enthusiasm that follows can lead to huge rewards. For Captain Guy Disney, it was becoming the first ever amputee to walk to both the North and South Poles. For Levison Wood, it was publishing his first travel book and documentary.

Eliza Rebeiro: A Passion to Help Others

Eliza Rebeiro couldn't have chosen a worse time to be a teenager in Croydon than during the first decade of the 21st century. Knife crime was so rife in the south London borough that it was dubbed 'the teen stabbing capital of Britain' by the national media. With crime so virulent, Eliza was inevitably drawn in. As a young teenager, she witnessed the brutal stabbing of three of her close friends: one slashed through the neck; another sliced across the chest; and a third stabbed in the back while police stood idly by only metres away.

In most instances, an arms race ensues with victims, understandably, arming themselves for protection. However, Eliza's response was different. At just thirteen years of age, she decided to fight back in a unique way. She set up Lives Not Knives – a local community group and charity organisation aimed at tackling the issue of knife crime.

Eliza's campaign began raising awareness through the manufacture and sale of t-shirts with the 'Lives Not Knives' slogan printed across the front. The t-shirts resonated so deeply with the local community that Eliza was soon able to expand production. With the proceeds, she went on to host a festival to celebrate young people having fun without violence. Once again, the event was a huge success as hundreds attended and signed a petition to support making the streets safer. Lives Not Knives was officially formed.

From its inception, Lives Not Knives has evolved from a community group, to a campaign and now into a fully-fledged charity, with board members and directors. In partnership with other charities, it works to mentor, educate and teach tens of thousands of school children and help prevent knife crime and deter children from joining a gang.

As the organisation has grown, so has Eliza. At the age of just fifteen she was actively leading the charity and giving talks to the community. By sixteen, she was meeting MPs in Parliament. Soon after, she was invited to present at City Hall to the Mayor of London, Boris Johnson, and give a speech at the Home Office.

Today, aged twenty-two, Eliza is a trained youth worker conducting conflict management workshops and violence workshops that address stereotyping, gang culture and numerous other issues. Despite her young age, Eliza has devoted one third of her life to Lives Not Knives and her efforts have been recognised by numerous awards, such as the Women of the Future Awards.

To have achieved so much, so young, is awe-inspiring. At the Lives Not Knives headquarters in Croydon, Eliza explains: "Motivating yourself is the most important thing. If you love what you do you will never work a day in your life. A job like mine is not a regular nine-to-five job, it requires your attention 24 hours a day." And when Eliza says 24 hours a day, she means it: after going out on an evening, she always comes home in the early hours and starts checking her e-mails. "I have got used to checking my e-mails at any time, whether it's 2am or 4am, because I don't want to miss an opportunity. You should make what you love part of your day until it becomes every minute of your day."

Eliza's success has come through hard work and determination: "At first, it was amazing, at age fifteen, to be talking to these people [the London Mayor and the Home Office] but two years later I realised nothing had happened. It was frustrating. Nothing was happening because young people don't have a vote. So, at the age of seventeen, I decided someone had to stand up and represent young people, so Lives Not Knives started working in schools and giving talks to young people aged nine to twenty-four. We would talk to young people about why they shouldn't get involved in gangs and what the dangers were. With the older children we tend to talk more about their experiences and how we can change things for them."

Everything that Eliza has accomplished shows a level of maturity and equanimity that belies her youth. From the depths of witnessing harrowing stabbings in Croydon, Eliza has built a constructive movement and has devoted herself to helping others. "I love working with young people, particularly in our Pupil Referral Units where I can witness the progress they have made. You have to enjoy exactly what you are doing and know exactly what you want to achieve. Role models are formed from people persisting in what they believe in."

Major Phil Ashby: A Passion for Adventure
Major Phil Ashby started an impressive career as the youngest commissioned officer in Her Majesty's Armed Forces aged seventeen and went on to become the youngest Major in the history of the entire Armed Forces by the age of just twenty-nine. Eventually, he completed Commando and Arctic Warfare

training, widely regarded as the longest and hardest specialist infantry course in the Armed Forces, to become an elite Royal Marines Mountain Leader.

Phil's unrelenting thirst for adventure and his unique capacity for endurance drove him to extraordinary achievements. Although his Marine Commando training involved covering 2,500 miles, completing 40,000 press-ups, 60,000 sit-ups, climbing 7,500 feet of rope and passing various cerebral tasks all in the space of just a few weeks, it was only the elite Mountain Leader training that pushed him to his physical and mental limit.

Eleven months long and so arduous that only a dozen men pass each year, it's almost impossible to describe the endurance needed for such a punishing programme. Phil recalls regular physical training sessions carrying fifty pound sandbags for up to four hours, which left recruits coughing up blood. Night exercise programmes could last ten days with no movement allowed during daylight. One training exercise involved a fifty mile trek with 120 pound backpacks, after which exhausted trainees were immediately blindfolded, stripped of all their kit and left for ten days on a remote island as a survival test. Any survivors were then ambushed at night and forced to endure Conduct After Capture training, where they were made to hold stress positions for up to thirty-six hours, then endure white noise for forty-eight hours to ensure sensory deprivation, before facing forty-eight hours of interrogation. Failing to resist interrogation meant expulsion from the course.

Phil's Royal Marines Mountain Leader training had made him a specialist in extreme cold weather and mountain combat but, ironically, his toughest survival challenge would be thrust upon him during a UN peacekeeping operation in Sierra Leone – one of the hottest places on earth.

It was May 2000 and Sierra Leone was lurching towards civil war. Phil was serving as the senior United Nations Disarmament and Decommissioning Officer in the region and he quickly became the top assassination target for the rebel RUF leader Colonel Bao. As civil war erupted, five hundred UN representatives were taken hostage with many tortured and killed. Phil found himself trapped inside a compound with colleagues, severely outnumbered and without a weapon.

Against the odds, Phil led his three fellow UN peacekeepers on an audacious escape. To survive, Phil and his team had to trek fifty miles in the searing heat, equipped with just one litre of water, a tin of baked beans, GPS, compass, map and a handful of water filtration tablets. The *British Military Handbook* states that troops are one hundred per cent ineffective after four days without sleep; Phil and his team stayed awake for just shy of a week. Incredibly, they managed to escape and Phil was awarded the Queen's Gallantry Medal for his remarkable efforts.

Today, Phil runs a successful climbing company in the Alps and, despite operating in different worlds, displays a strikingly similar belief and drive to charity founder Eliza Rebeiro.

"The people who do the best in life are the people who have been able to choose their niche rather than have something imposed upon them," Phil says. "Identify what *you* want to do and not what your parents, your friends, society or teachers want. Ultimately, you must have the courage of your convictions to pursue the things you want. If you end up in the wrong job, you may have some success in the short term but, in the long term, you will not. If you combine the right job with a feeling of satisfaction, it's easy to be a success."

Phil continues, "My motivation has always been – and it's a line I've adapted for my book and speeches – that I've always been a bit of an adrenaline junkie, but that there's no high to be had like the feeling that you're doing a good job, especially if it's a good job which makes a difference. Although jumping out of a plane is great, it doesn't last very long. Whereas setting up your own little business and nurturing it and watching it become a success is just as big a kick, and, in many respects, a lot harder to pull off."

Like Eliza Rebeiro, the reward for his endeavours is more than financial. "If you're doing something where, in some small way, you're making the world a better place, then the motivation is easy," he says. "I was honoured when the Queen pinned a medal on my chest. I can honestly say that that meant more to me than being given a large financial bonus or anything similar. In the military you're never going to get rich but, nonetheless, that feeling of pride when you're rewarded in other ways is fantastic. It's worth millions of pounds in itself."

Although Phil is no longer in the army, he finds the same sense of purpose in his climbing business. "Mountain guiding is not making the world a better place but you're having such a positive impact on people who are probably in stressful and demanding jobs with only two weeks of holiday a year," he says. "They've chosen to spend a fair bit of money in order to come and climb a mountain with me and I get such a kick from showing these people a really good time. This summer I had the world's most reserved Englishman, who had tried to climb the Matterhorn about ten times over the last thirty years and never got to the top. When I eventually got him to the top, he had a tear in his eye and, completely out of character, gave me a massive hug. I felt like the best person in the world. It was just an amazing feeling."

Although operating in vastly different worlds, Phil and Eliza allude to the pressure from society and peers. "At such a young age, it takes a lot of certainty to identify what it is that you want to do, as opposed to what your parents, your friends, your teachers or society want you to do," he admits. "I think the people who do best in life are those who, through luck or design, have been able to choose their niche rather than do something that was forced upon them by someone else."

What was Phil's motivation in the face of such life-threatening danger in Sierra Leone? "I suspect that I am relatively lucky in that I've always been comfortable with danger," he reveals. "There's nothing much more thrilling than being shot at. While I was escaping capture in Sierra Leone, I got a real thrill from the fact that the training was worthwhile and I was good at dealing with the situation I was facing. I was extremely scared but I was also very aware that I was experiencing a real life scenario that a lot of my colleagues would never get to experience."

For Phil, the more difficult motivational challenge has always been when the situation has been calm. "The hardest thing is trying to motivate people around you when it's not a life-or-death situation," he says. "That may sound counterintuitive but if people are shooting at you then it's remarkably easy to motivate the people around you – if you don't do your job properly then you're unlikely to make it out alive. My hardest leadership challenge was when I did a three month tour in Northern Ireland during the 1997 ceasefire. I was with a group of Paratroopers – famous for being good soldiers but, frankly, not always the best diplomats in the world. It was a politically sensitive time when the British government didn't want to have any British soldiers being seen out and about. Nonetheless, being with paras confined to barracks was akin to being with a group of disgruntled and caged animals who felt both severely under-stimulated and under-appreciated. Trying to convince them that they were still doing a great job while also keeping them occupied with training and planning, I found to be a surprisingly massive challenge."

Ironically, banal situations which are not life or death seem to be somewhat challenging for Phil. "My wife always gives me a hard time about it," he laughs. "She can't believe I've got the Queen's Gallantry Medal, yet won't make a cold call to the garage to ask them for a quote on the car. Of course, if push comes to shove, I can do it, so I guess it's not that I'm scared of it, but ..." To get round this, Phil draws on his army training. "There's a military phrase that is apt: instructors or superiors will often say 'have a word with yourself' when you're not pulling your weight. I've learnt to be able to do that and kick myself up the proverbial backside and get on with it."

Despite the temptation, Phil knows the rewards that come from pursuing his *passion*. "If I'm not active or if I'm not working hard, be that physical or mental, I feel guilty when it comes to relaxing," he says. "In fact, I have never slept as well as I did when I was in basic marine training."

Phil has more than earned his rewards over a stellar career and has myriad experiences, good and bad, to draw on if feeling in need of motivation. "You only live once and I think it's a lot more fun if you're able to see the positives," he says. "For example, it's easy to become cynical if you spend several months in hospital (Phil was hospitalised with an inflamed spinal cord on his return from Sierra Leone) thinking you might not ever be able to walk again, or if you don't have proper use of your bladder when you are able to walk again, or when you realise you will be pushing paper for the rest of your career because they won't allow you back on the front line. Or you can try and see the positives. In my case, I became aware that I was learning to be a nicer and a better person having previously not been the most sympathetic person in the world. My emotional intelligence and sympathy for others grew massively after being in a hospital and being surrounded by people who were in a much worse condition than me."

As with Captain Guy Disney, Phil knows all too well the challenges and rewards of recovery following hospitalisation. "They wouldn't let me out of hospital until I could walk to the loo on my own," Phil explains. "Walking the fifty feet to the hospital toilet was harder than doing fifty miles in the jungle, yet nobody would think you were Superman for walking to the loo solo. So, ultimately, your eyes open and you suddenly feel connected to so many people."

It's hard to not be in awe of the achievements of Eliza and Phil. Each of them has an intrinsic motivation that drives what they do and, importantly, any pecuniary reward has simply come as a function of following their *passion*. Yet, despite their successes, it is the more mortal elements of their characters which intrigue. The reality that Phil was able to escape death at the hands of gun-toting warlords by only a whisker yet struggles to ring his local mechanic for a quote is comfortingly human.

Chapter 3

Passion: Innate vs Evolving

Evidently, *passion* unleashes huge amounts of commitment, focus, devotion and enthusiasm – amounts that can lead to immense rewards. Rather than just illustrating the importance of *passion*, it is vital to delineate the different sources of *passion*. Is it innate or does it evolve? Where does this elusive enthusiasm emanate from? For some, *passion* is in their DNA.

Innate Passion: John Neill, Michael Acton-Smith and Linzi Boyd

John Neill is one of the UK's leading businessmen and has led Unipart Manufacturing Logistics and Consulting for over thirty years, making him the longest serving CEO of any major company in Europe. In that time, he has taken Unipart from the brink of bankruptcy and on to becoming one of the ten largest privately owned companies in the country. Under his leadership, Unipart turns over in excess of £1 billion per annum and employs five times more people than when he began as CEO. Back in the 1980s, Unipart's customer base was just two clients, now the company works with thousands of businesses across the globe, including the likes of Vodafone, Sky and Siemens.

John cut his business teeth at automotive manufacturer General Motors before moving to rival British Leyland, then the parent company of Unipart. State owned British Leyland once produced iconic cars such as the Mini Cooper, Range Rover and E-type Jaguar, to name a few, but when John was appointed CEO in 1976, the company was in a state of paralysis due to militant trade union strikes. At the age of just twenty-nine, John was tasked with rescuing a business that was in the middle of a strike costing the company half a million pounds a day (equivalent to £5 million per day in today's money).

John's journey started at a much earlier age, at a time when he was single-minded about what he wanted to do, despite his parents' wishes. "When I was twelve, I decided I wanted to be a businessman," he reveals. "In a way, I'm sure I was heavily influenced by my father. He was a great entrepreneur but he tried to deter me from being a businessman and recommended I become a doctor or an engineer. He definitely didn't try to get me to follow in his footsteps but, nonetheless, I always had huge admiration for him."

John's father wasn't the only dissenting voice in his career choice. "I went to school in Scotland and, when I mentioned I wanted to be a businessman, my parents' friends would always suggest I became a teacher or doctor," he remembers. "I would always stand my ground and tell them how I wanted to run my own business. Business is what I wanted to do, so I went to Strathclyde University to do a business degree. If one couldn't become a brain surgeon unless one studied brain surgery, then, by the same logic, one couldn't become a businessman unless one had learned about marketing, economics, law, accounting and so on. So I did that and continued on to do an MBA. I went to General Motors because they paid for me to do the MBA. They paid me a salary on condition that I went to work for them afterwards, which I did."

John's *passion* to succeed in business was put to the test on his arrival at British Leyland and his response was uncompromising. "In my opinion, it was an awful and toxic place to work," he admits. "People were unhappy and the unions were intimidating. I knew the company had to be run by me and not the Industrial Relations department or unions. I was going to get the workers to come back and work hard, like I did. I worked hard and so did all my team; we all worked twelve hours a day and we loved it."

Yet John never felt overwhelmed by the challenge. "I knew what we had to do and we were going to do it my way or they would need to find someone else to run the business," he says. "I wasn't prepared to manage it the way it had been. Did I have any doubts? No, because it was the right thing to do."

In a sense, John's business career was forged from his teenage rebellion against his father's advice. "From the day I arrived here [Unipart] I was continually told I couldn't change things," he says. "I just hope I get more right than wrong." Despite running the company for three decades, he still loves his work. John echoed the famous quote about finding a job you like and never having to work a day in your life. For all John's success, his drive is still ferocious. "I'll never be satisfied," he explains. "Yes, I'm happy but, no, I'm never satisfied. You might be happy but you shouldn't be satisfied because then you stop striving."

"I'm not driven by money as some people in business are," **Michael Acton-Smith** mentions at his company offices – an eye-popping fusion of Hansel and Gretel and Willy Wonka-esque design. "There's nothing wrong with it," he continues, "but it's not the key driver for me."

Michael Acton-Smith is the founder of the entertainment company Mind Candy and creator of the global phenomenon *Moshi Monsters* – an online game where players adopt a personalised pet monster. The game is played by a staggering 80 million users worldwide. Following its online success, *Moshi Monsters* expanded into physical products including toys, a music album, a video game, trading cards and even a feature film. Mind Candy also produces other online games for kids such as *PopJam*, known as the 'Instagram for kids', which allows users to create and share art, stories, photos and games. It's most recent hit is *World of Warriors*, a thematic combat strategy game that has generated millions of downloads on mobile app stores.

Michael is someone whose enthusiasm and *passion* for what he does is apparent from the moment you shake his hand. "I think the drive comes down to my love of ideas, making things, trying things and being creative," he says. "I think business is the perfect canvas to test out ideas because the marketplace is the ultimate decider of whether something is a good or bad idea. It will either work or it won't and I find that fascinating. I don't know where it comes from but my brain is always whirring and thinking up new things. What drives me is trying new stuff."

As with John Neill, the sense of enjoyment that Michael gets from work is infectious. Indeed, he doesn't see what he does as work, in the traditional sense. "I don't know whether it's school, one's upbringing or something else, but so many people go through life assuming work has to be something that is unenjoyable and something you have to get through to do all the other fun stuff in life," he says. "But if you are spending most of your waking hours and energy at a place of work then you should make it something that fascinates and interests you. I think it's extremely important to do work that you love." He continues, "often, the rebuke is that it's not possible to make money from passions. There is some truth to that but, nonetheless, I think if you go deep into something that you love, there are ways, especially in the age of the internet, to reach an audience or generate revenue from it. I think the world would be a much happier place if people did that."

Michael's success with *Moshi Monsters* was not an overnight success. Mind Candy's first product wasn't a hit. "*Perplex City* was a wonderfully ambitious and creative game with a set of stories and puzzles," he remembers. "We had a small audience who were very passionate about it but it didn't go mainstream.

It was just too complex." Michael had to take the difficult decision to close down the game and tell his investors it hadn't worked. Meanwhile, he already had the idea for *Moshi Monsters*, but to develop it required a total rethink of the company. "It was very tough and stressful to pivot the entire business," he says. "We had to let people go and rebuild the team again from scratch."

As *Moshi Monsters* was being developed, the credit crunch and financial difficulties threatened to derail everything. "I couldn't get a meeting with anyone and we had run out of cash by December [2008] so couldn't even meet payroll," he reveals. "That was scary because, as an entrepreneur, you have a huge responsibility for people's livelihoods. I had many sleepless nights. I didn't know what I was going to do." Remarkably, at the eleventh hour, Michael found an investor and took the bold leap of shifting *Moshi Monsters* from a freemium model to a subscription one and the success was almost immediate. "We stood around the computer waiting to see what would happen and, within the first five minutes, we had our first payment," he says. "Then seconds later we had our second and third. We came back in the morning and we had already generated thousands of pounds of revenue. That month we made about £25,000 and then £50,000 the next month and we never looked back."

Undoubtedly, the depth of Michael's *passion* for what he was trying to do was instrumental in motivating both himself and his team through the more difficult moments of the company's early gestation. "As an entrepreneur, you've got to have a lot of resilience and perseverance to go through all the sleepless nights and self-doubt that starts creeping in when, month by month, you trudge onwards and still don't find the magic formula," he says. "If you believe in your vision and you are pig-headed enough, you can plough through until you eventually find that magic."

The psychological arm-wrestle between self-belief and doubt is a daily struggle. "Everyone has an inner critic that is constantly chipping away and allowing self-doubt in – the key is to just try and override it," he advises. "This is why a lot of the best entrepreneurs seem to be a bit delusional or even bonkers – they try to solve problems when everyone else thinks it's crazy. Often the best and biggest ideas are the ones that don't seem immediately obvious. They're almost counterintuitive. You have to be strong-willed and believe in yourself and your vision. No matter how many bumps in the road or obstacles you have to get around, you keep on going."

Unlike John Neill's persistent confidence, Michael admits that his tends to fluctuate. "In general, I think I have a lot of confidence and self-belief but it definitely wavers from time to time," he admits. "We've been working on a new product called *PopJam* – the next big thing after *Moshi Monsters* – for two years now and haven't really seen any magic yet. I believe there is something huge here, but two years is a long time and it's expensive. We've got a big team and many people have come and gone since we started. But because I feel so strongly that this will be an industry-changing and multi-billion dollar product, I'm willing to keep charging forward because, at some point, we will crack it."

Linzi Boyd is a businesswoman with *passion* to spare. "From a young age, I used to tell my mother I was going to be as big as Oprah Winfrey, while my mum used to look at me with a quizzical expression. I've always had this vision to develop brands and do it my own way."

Her mother didn't roll her eyes for long – Linzi knew what she wanted to do and set about it. "At the age of fourteen, I used to go into town on Saturdays and go to one specific shop and ask them for a job," she says. "Every Saturday. For an entire year. At the end of the ninth month of going into the store, the manager gave me a job as a Saturday girl. On my first Saturday I smashed all of their sales records."

Linzi knew that retail and brands were her calling but leaving school early was a challenge. "Although they put me in the top sets at school, it was not my world. I wasn't happy," she remembers. "I was determined, bright and wanted to learn, but I wasn't learning what I wanted to learn." Support eventually came from her boss. "At the age of fifteen, when I was about to take my GCSEs, my boss took my dad out and persuaded him to let me leave school. My dad was a dentist and came from an academic background, so to persuade him to let me leave school was quite an ordeal. Even my brother was studying dentistry!"

Linzi's father was eventually persuaded and her career took off. "Aged eighteen, I opened up the first women's shop in Leeds that sold brands like Replay and Diesel," she says. "At the time the Leeds United football team was huge. Eric Cantona, Vinnie Jones, Gary McAllister and Gary Speed all played for Leeds and they all used to come into my shop with their wives. The shop did really well."

Two years later, Linzi headed to London where she set up a footwear brand with Justin Deakin called Stride. "We sold 150,000 pairs in the first season, which was phenomenal," she recalls. "I was twenty-one at the time and we had Robbie Williams and the Beastie Boys wearing the shoes. We even got them into the Design Museum as a design classic." At twenty-four, Linzi sold the company to shoe company Caterpillar and founded the Surgery Group – an agency that creates and 'refreshes' local and global brands. Superdry, Pringle, Wrangler, Urban Outfitters, Givenchy, Lacoste and Rankin are just some of the household names she has launched and revived.

It's a remarkable success story and one achieved with little self-doubt. "I have always worked on the premise – 'Do it, then learn it'," she says. "I wasn't going to be a dentist like my brother and father because that wasn't my path. You know in your heart what you can and cannot do and, even though I didn't know a thing about textbook marketing, I knew I could do it. I came from running two businesses and transferred the knowledge of being an entrepreneur to help brands create growth and scale. Now, I've set up the Business of Brand School and written a book called *Brand Famous*. The BoB School is now running in the UK, Canada and Australia to help the next generation of business leaders create brand fame."

Linzi describes *passion* as being part of her DNA. "I always say everything is within your DNA. You are your brand and your brand is you, so passion will run through absolutely everything that you do. If not, the likelihood is you're going to give up. When I don't accomplish things, it's probably because it's not sitting with the true me."

*   *   *

Evolving Passion: Kirsty Henderson and Roz Savage

Linzi Boyd, Michael Acton-Smith and John Neill, have a *passion* for their careers that oozes from every pore and that propelled them from an early age. However, for martial artist **Kirsty Henderson** and ocean rower **Roz Savage**, their *passion* emerged later in life.

Standing just a little over five feet tall with a diminutive physique but cheery disposition, Kirsty Henderson doesn't come across as a stereotypical world champion martial artist. More specifically, she is a Blackbelt 3rd Dan in Mixed Martial Arts (MMA) and a Blackbelt 2nd Dan in Shidokan karate. She is also a qualified instructor in Krav Maga, Specialist Defence and Knives & Edged Weapons for the UK Martial Arts Alliance. Impressively, Kirsty was British Champion and ranked number one in the world for Shidokan karate for the majority of her fighting career.

Despite all her achievements, Kirsty's early goal was in a different field – she wanted to become an architect. It required a Bachelor's degree, time spent training in an architect's practice, an Honours degree, a professional diploma and final professional exams. As a result, Kirsty had little time left for anything else. "In architecture, there's no time for anything," she says. "I was swimming for relaxation, but we were always working. My concentration was principally on my architecture course."

It wasn't until Kirsty moved to London and completed her architecture qualifications that she picked up martial arts formally. "I had started working at a company and one of the guys on the team was training at this fight club," she remembers. "He would come into the office with the odd black eye, limping and stinking of Tiger Balm. I asked if I could tag along. He refused and explained that it was not a commercial club, but a family run club between London and Japan."

Kirsty continues, "It took about six months to persuade him to take me along. It was round the back of King's Cross railway station, down a cobbled street – past the prostitutes and everything – and then up some rickety stairs in an old warehouse. It was a dusty place with bags hanging everywhere; there wasn't anything else like it at the time. The guy teaching was a twenty-one-year-old black belt who had just come back from Japan. He was as hard as nails and I started training straight away and got really into it. It was tough but I became hooked. I quickly started to go through grading and realised that I was good at it and one thing just led to another."

Kirsty was hooked on Shidokan karate; an unusual choice for a finely built girl. Shidokan is a test of extreme physical endurance and requires intense power to defeat opponents. The bouts are simply bare knuckle knockdowns. Fights are not won by scoring points or striking certain body areas rather, the victory goes to the competitor who is first to floor their opponent. The fights can last seconds or minutes and no padding is permitted. The aim is to strike your opponent and finish the fight as quickly as possible.

To become a black belt in Shidokan karate Kirsty had to compete in violent bouts as part of the curriculum and gradings. "The black belts for Shidokan are demanding," she says. "I did two different ten-man fights for my first black belt and a fourteen-man fight for my second. There are no gloves – it is full contact and the next fighter comes in after the other. But the fights are only part of it and are nestled amongst hours of endurance training." In Kirsty's case, the endurance element of her black belt assessment in Japan included cleaning the entire dojo with a face cloth for around four hours, followed by a 5.5 kilometre race up a mountain against some of Japan's top male fighters. "I came fifth out of twenty, the only girl of course, and then it was straight back into the dojo for a fourteen-man kumite (fight)," she says. "Having just beaten fifteen of the men in the race they were very happy to get their revenge – I have never been hit so hard in my life! Then, when we finished with the fights, we went straight into three hours of working on our drills and sequences."

Kirsty was the first and, to this day, the only female Shidokan black belt from Great Britain. Her exceptional fighting skills and resilience left an enduring impression in Japan. Following her fourteen-man fight she was ranked as the top female fighter in the world by Grand Master Kancho Yoshiji Seono. He described Kirsty as "the best female fighter he has ever seen at anytime and anywhere in the world." A further accolade was bestowed on Kirsty in Japan after she attained her second black belt; for the ceremonial dinner that followed she was positioned next to Grand Master Kancho, a rare honour for a female from the West. At the end of the dinner, as a gesture of respect, one of the Shihans that she had defeated approached Kirsty, removed his shirt and presented it to her. "Karate flows through her," Grand Master Kancho pithily puts it. Despite discovering her *passion* later in life, Kirsty is a vivid illustration of what is possible when passions are pursued.

"A bad day on the water is still better than a good day in the office," goes the old surfer saying, but, for **Roz Savage**, it took many years for her to discover the truth behind the maxim.

In many respects, Roz Savage's life had been a sequence of successes. She read Law at University College Oxford and went on to work as a management consultant in the City for blue-chip firms such as Andersen Consulting (now Accenture), CHP Consulting and UBS. While working as a consultant, she met and married Richard, who also worked at Andersen Consulting, and, together, they seemed the epitome of the high-flying career couple. Roz's choice of profession was rooted in a teenage visit to America on an exchange trip to San Diego that introduced her to materialism and consumerism, a far cry from her modest upbringing under the watchful eye of her Methodist minister father. Eventually a successful career in the City seemed to give her everything she desired.

Except, peculiarly, Roz's work life was not giving her the satisfaction she had expected. "I had clung for far too long to the illusion that material things were going to bring me joy," she says. "This illusion had blinded me to the simple truth that happiness is a state of mind and that not even all the riches under the sun could make me a happy person." Once, on her commute into work on a cramped train, Roz found herself staring at the obituary page of a newspaper and it got her thinking. That evening she decided to write two obituaries for herself – one of the life she was living at present and one of the life she wanted to live.

"It felt so vivid and authentic when I was writing that fantasy obituary," Roz says, "even though I was scared of what I had just glimpsed, I think I realised it meant that I'd been barking up the wrong tree in terms of what a successful life looked like. That was embarrassing to admit and I think I suspected that it would have implications for my marriage. I recognised that my husband was not going to come with me on that journey towards the person that I wanted to be so deeply and it was scary to even begin to imagine how I would get myself on course for that life. At the same time, I think it's one of those things that once you know it, you can't un-know it. It's there."

For the first time, Roz sensed what would become her driving *passion*: "It made me believe in the power of having a vision of where you want to end up, because, once you have that vision, it takes root and subconsciously starts to govern the choices you make. I subconsciously sabotaged my comfortable life so that I actually had to get out there, be more adventurous, independent and self-reliant."

What Roz wanted was adventure and, although she had done some rowing when she was at university, she had never attempted anything like what she was about to do next and become the first solo woman ever to enter the Atlantic Rowing Race. Roz's Atlantic row was a remarkable journey of just under 3,000 miles, which she managed in 103 days, five hours and forty-three minutes, while pulling about 1,000,000 oar strokes in the process. Since then, she has continued to row remarkable distance after remarkable distance: from San Francisco to Hawaii in 2008 (2,324 miles), Hawaii to Kiribati in 2009 (3,158 miles), Kiribati to Papua New Guinea in 2010 (2,248 miles) and from Australia to Mauritius in 2011 (over 3,500 miles).

"I look back at when I was a young adult and think I did things because I cared too much about what other people thought of me," Roz says. "To get over that has been hugely empowering. I don't think I'm any different from the next person, but I've surprised myself by what I can put up with."

There is no definitive answer to whether *passion* is innate or learnt. For some, *passion* is evident when they are barely in their teens and it feels part of their DNA. For others, it emerges later in life. What is clear is how paramount that sense of intrinsic motivation is. The word *passion* is derived from the Latin word *passio* meaning suffering or enduring. As we will see with Gilo Cardozo, *passion* is the precursor to an intense sense of focus which lays the foundations for the second trait, *grit*.

Chapter 4

Case Study – Gilo Cardozo

"I didn't have to think about what I wanted to do. I just had a compulsion to make stuff." As a young boy tinkering with engines in his garden shed, Gilo Cardozo knew exactly what he wanted to spend his life doing, he says, "I want to make stuff that propels humans around, whether it's on the water, on the ground, in the air or in outer space. But particularly airborne machines as they are a very exciting challenge."

With an MBE to his name, Gilo is the founder and Chief Technology Officer of Gilo Industries Group. The group has manufactured thousands of Parajet paramotors (engine powered-paragliders) and has invented the world's first road legal flying car, the SkyCar.

His singular focus and obsession with his work is evident at his research facility in Dorset as he recalls his early career when he invested the royalties from his first product, the LadderMax, into setting up Parajet and developing his engine powered-paraglider. "It was over three years before I had a reliable machine and in that time I did almost nothing else but work on that machine," he recounts. "If I look back, I don't think I could have done any more than I did. I regularly worked through the night and the concept of weekends didn't really exist. I wanted to make it absolutely brilliant, absolutely perfect."

Gilo was attempting to achieve something single-handedly that most companies tackled with teams of engineers and extensive capital investment. The shortfall he made up was in the hours he was willing to commit. "I was doing most of it on my own and that's one of the reasons why it was hard," he says. "I was amazed by how much more it took than I expected. If I look back to the period when I built the first machine, I had rebuilt, redesigned parts and mended bits thousands of times. The thought of how many times I have turned a spanner round is crazy. If I was working on a factory line however, I would likely be doing repetitive work every day so I always count myself very lucky."

But as Gilo's devotion to his machines became almost monastic, his social life soon began to suffer. "Although I love the idea of being able to stop working when a great invitation comes along, I actually found I preferred to stay in my workshop, all night if needed, to get things done," he admits. "I wanted to perfect my machine way more than go drinking with friends. I was turning things down left, right and centre because that is what it took to get the engine and Parajet to work. I just had this innate, intense passion for making this brilliant machine and it meant that everything else became less important."

That level of devotion didn't tail off once his invention was ready for sale. The attention Gilo gave to people buying his first Parajet motors manifested itself in customer service par excellence. Gilo would regularly drive all over the country and even take flights abroad to visit customers with his toolbox. He camped outside customers' houses, sleeping in tents or in fields, to ensure their machine was fixed by the following day. "It sounds crazy but I was learning on the job," he says. "The idea of being able to get people flying these machines that I had built and seeing the smile on their faces when they had landed, was more important than anything else at the time. It was all part of what I was trying to build and more important than money, which was just a means to make the next machine and expand our capabilities."

Today, Gilo Industries is a successful business where the dedication to the product remains paramount. "It wasn't about making money, it was about making fantastic products," he stresses. "Turning these chunks of metal into something beautiful and exciting allowed me to keep going and make more beautiful things that could make money to pay for the next ones to be built." Gilo reinvested the profits from Parajet into expanding and developing the customer experience by establishing a Parajet flying school in Cyprus. With a suitable climate and reliable weather, he invested in hiring instructors and has now successfully expanded the market for paramotoring.

In short, Gilo has redefined the capabilities of both paramotors and ultra light-weight aero engines by incorporating high tech composite materials, refined geometry and digital engine managements systems in order to optimise every element of the product. To put the new technology firmly on the map, Gilo designed a new personal aircraft to fly higher than any before. In May 2007, Gilo and renowned explorer Bear Grylls flew from the base of the Himalayas and over the summit of Everest at a height of 29,494ft to set a new world record for paramotoring.

Gilo Cardozo's achievements are the result of tens of thousands of hours devoted to relentlessly pursuing a *passion* and his company mission statement reflects this: "Each company thrives on going beyond the bounds of what was previously thought possible." Gilo's flying car invention, the SkyCar, is a case in point. The SkyCar is part all-terrain vehicle and part light aircraft or, in other words, a beach buggy with a paraglider wing that allows it to take-off and land on almost any terrain. To prove its unique flying and driving credentials the car completed a gruelling 7,000 kilometre expedition from London to Timbuktu, flying over the Straits of Gibraltar and the Sahara in the process.

But what is the key trait that drives everything Gilo has accomplished? "It's an underlying self confidence that you are right and your vision is not mad even when other people don't get it," he reflects. "It is not something that you consciously think about, it's something that is plugging away even when things aren't going to plan. In many ways, I think it's pure luck if you know what you want to do. Some people advocate that you make you're own luck but I am not convinced by that theory. I never decided to be fascinated by making flying machines, I was just naturally very excited about it, so much so that I couldn't consider doing anything else and any hardship experienced along the way is part of the journey and should, wherever possible be embraced. I feel very lucky because I enjoy what I am doing so much. I'm following a dream."

Trait 2
GRIT

Chapter 1

Case Study: James Rhodes

"People think if they haven't nailed it in a week there is no point continuing. They start to write a book or play an instrument or begin an art course and they realise, after a week, they are not Picasso or that they don't have an eighty thousand word novel in them so they just give up. To produce one album takes me thousands and thousands of hours of practise. People often don't realise it takes years of pain, heartbreak and stress and you have to really want something for it to succeed."

Grit is the insatiable inclination to toil and persist. It is the focus, persistence and commitment to achieve a chosen goal and the *Great Britons* who possess it are dogged and relentless.

James Rhodes has released six piano albums and regularly tops the iTunes classical music charts. He has played to thousands of fans around the world and is also a newspaper columnist, television presenter and bestselling author.

However, James is no ordinary pianist. He has turned the traditional perception and stereotype of a concert pianist on its head with performances and a style that are unique in the staid world of classical music. He rose to prominence through a number of extraordinary circumstances after suffering sexual abuse as a young boy, attempting to take his own life and spending time in – and even escaping – a psychiatric hospital.

To endure all that and achieve musical success has required a huge amount of persistence, commitment and, above all, *grit*.

"I didn't go the normal route," James reflects from the drawing room in his Maida Vale flat where his piano takes pride of place. "Normally a concert pianist, with almost no exceptions, starts at three or four years old, occasionally a little bit later, and by the time they're eighteen the technique, the repertoire and everything else is all there. Then they may go to music college and then do competitions. But, as far as the technical facility is concerned, they are fully formed. It's a bit like a 100 metre sprinter; they don't just start when they're thirty and overweight and end up winning Olympic gold."

James, on the other hand, was the opposite of conventional. "I got my first proper teacher when I was fourteen, and then at eighteen I stopped playing for ten years," he reveals. At the age of eighteen, James was offered a scholarship to the Guildhall School of Music but, to his chagrin, his parents insisted he pursued a more traditional university education. "They were adamant I should have a proper career, that was more diverse and would open up more doors," he says. "At that age I didn't have the balls to defy them." James was forced to abandon his dream of becoming a pianist. Instead, he graduated with a degree in psychology and stumbled into a job in financial publishing that he loathed. "It was an awful place and had absolutely no redeeming qualities whatsoever, apart from the income," he says. "I would see people working there in their forties and fifties and just think that, if that was me in twenty years, I should be shot."

James became convinced that it was too late to fulfil his piano dreams. "I was listening to music all the time and knew it was what I really wanted," he says. "I made this terrible mistake of thinking that if I hadn't done it by a certain age, I would never do it and so I gave up. It was only at the age of twenty-eight that I thought, actually, I *can* do it."

Even then, James's change of chosen career came by chance. "I was going to become an agent because I thought I'd live vicariously through other pianists," he recalls. "I quit my job and found an agent based in Italy who looked after the greatest living pianists. I thought I should learn from the best so we were put in touch and he invited me over to Verona to learn the ropes for a couple of weeks. While I was there he asked if I played the piano and I explained that I hadn't for ten years. He then asked for me to play him something and, after I did, he said: 'I've never heard anyone play like that who isn't a professional pianist. You're not going to be an agent. You'll come every month and you'll study with a friend of mine who's the best teacher in Italy.' So I did that for five years, working non-stop."

His teacher, Edoardo Strabbioli, was a man James describes, with a wry smile. "In my opinion he was aggressive, humiliating, and horrifically critical about everything." James continues, "but that was what I needed as he pulled everything apart and started afresh. Although I wouldn't put anyone else through that because I almost didn't make it myself; it was painful.

"Edoardo is a brilliant pianist, but, primarily, he is a phenomenal teacher. He showed me things that you could never learn in books or figure out on your own – I mean specific little tricks, tips and methods that are passed down from teacher to pupil over the generations. That opened the gates for me because it showed me that, no matter how difficult I thought the piece was or how far beyond my technical abilities I thought it was, with the right kind of practise it was always possible to pull something off."

Practise is fundamental to the success of a musician, irrespective of an innate musical ability. "No matter how old you are, or what skills you have, there's no question in my mind that with a piano, the right teacher, the right frame of mind and an hour of practise a day, you can be a success," James says. "It's a question of logic and physics. You can learn everything there is about how to physically play the piano in about an hour and then you just need to learn how to apply it."

James describes his daily practise routine as "no more than four hours and it's very deliberate and careful. A lot will depend on what I'm doing – if I'm memorising a full piece or if I'm just learning the notes, or whether it's a new or an old piece. But some things are consistent: there's a pencil, a metronome, an ashtray and a cup of coffee. And then it's just page by page, stopping whenever there's a physically difficult passage, and just hammering away at it until you can get through it and move on. It's not rocket science, just very methodical."

James shows the importance of *passion*, outlined in section one, and how this is an effective precursor to developing *grit*. When asked if there are ever days he can't be bothered to practise he retorts, "No – I never have days like that. I do have plenty of days where I think I'm playing like crap and it's a lost cause and I want to throw myself out of the window. But even when I've been told by a doctor to take a few days off, by 8.30 pm the same day I'm back at the piano."

James's commitment to his piano playing, along with his overall persistence, are vividly illustrated by countless moments throughout his life. For example, his decision to renounce his City publishing career and pursue his *passion* at an immeasurable cost to his regular life. "I quit my job and resigned myself to five years without an income and lost almost everything – my money, my house, my marriage, my health and my dignity," he admits. "It was a huge gamble but I knew that if I didn't do it like that, I wouldn't do it at all as I'd give up and go back to what was safe and secure, even if it was miserable." Having made the decision to change, James was determined to play the game by his own rules, as anyone fortunate enough to see him perform would testify to. "I think the thing I'm most proud of is sticking to my guns from the get-go," he says. "I wasn't going to wear a white tie and tails and go down the normal concert route. Instead, I wanted to wear jeans, chat to the audience, play at different kinds of venues and make my own way."

James's determination to overcome the fear that arises from performing live concerts is another illustration of his *grit*. "The thing I've found the hardest is the constant self-doubt because it impacts everything," he says. "I get stressed and that impacts things, from stage fright to nerves, but it's getting easier with experience. If I had been performing from the age of six, by twenty it would be just another day at the office, whereas it has been only five years since I first started performing. It's a huge thing to suddenly get your head around. You've often got 2,000 people who've paid money to come and hear you play 120,000 notes from memory, and it's probably being recorded, filmed or broadcast live on the radio while there are most likely critics in the audience. It's a giant thing to be able to somehow get through, let alone enjoy it and do well."

Undoubtedly, the biggest challenge James has faced has been a more personal one. In his memoir *Instrumental* he describes the horrific abuse he suffered as a young boy, as well as the demons of breakdown and addiction he has had to cope with since. James's achievements would be remarkable enough on their own but the fact that he has achieved them and dealt with these personal challenges at the same time makes it clear what an extraordinary individual he is. *Grit* is at his very core.

Chapter 2

Commitment and Persistence

Depending on the circumstances, *grit* can manifest itself in different forms. It can be the dedication and focus to master a *passion* or skill via thousands of hours of practise. It can be determination and doggedness in the face of adversity. Or *grit* can be the drive to embrace an opportunity.

James Rhodes is an individual who embodies all of these forms. The commitment to refine his *passion* for the piano is clear, as was his overcoming of adversity, from suffering abuse as a child and starting his music career late in life to, finally, his determination to embrace the opportunity to travel to Italy and learn from a great mentor. Equally, in conjunction with their *passion*, the *Great Britons* in part one displayed *grit* in abundance.

An explorer, a former member of the Special Forces and a renowned tutor, all from different walks of life, personify these various forms of *grit*.

"When I decided to become a tutor I had no idea of the life that awaited me: from the amazing places I have travelled to, right through to the inspiring people I've met. I've had the great fortune to be the guest of world leaders and even jam with musicians who were my idols as I was growing up."

Despite the legal confidentiality clauses, **Mark Maclaine** has built a reputation as one of the most prolific one-to-one tutors in the world in mathematics and science. Mark's pupils have included the children of royal families, sports stars, movie stars, musicians and billionaires. He can be found tutoring in

London, Hong Kong, Cannes, St Moritz, New York and the Caribbean. Mark is also the co-founder of Tutorfair, a company which sources tutors for parents and students, and has established the Tutorfair Foundation to provide free tuition for children who can't afford it via its innovative one-for-one model.

For all the privilege of many of Mark's wealthy students, his own childhood was very different. "I grew up in council housing," Mark recalls, "and my parents weren't particularly wealthy. I was born in South Africa and we left when I was about five or six. A lot of people were leaving because of Apartheid and, at the time, you couldn't take any money out of the country, not that we really had any anyway. My mum, my sister and I moved to London and, for a while, we lived in a tiny little room that we shared. Eventually the council gave us a flat and that's where I lived up until I was about twenty or so. We were pretty poor. So we relied on our family to help us."

Mark describes the uncomfortable contrast with wealthy members of his extended family. "We would holiday in European castles belonging to our cousins who were European aristocracy. We'd visit these beautiful places that often had servants, so it wasn't a pleasant experience having to then go back to our flat and wonder why we weren't able to have that too."

This led to Mark questioning himself and not believing he was good enough, compounded further by his father's death while he was still young.

Ironically, given his subsequent career choice, Mark struggled with his formal education. "I wasn't great at school," he admits. "I had a lot of anger issues and was diagnosed with Attention Deficit Hyperactivity Disorder (ADHD). The only things I was good at were mathematics and science because my dyslexia meant that writing was always difficult for me."

Mark became particularly adept with computers and ended up studying computer science. "When I was eight years old we found a broken computer in a skip," he remembers. "My grandfather was able to fix it for me and I taught myself how to programme on it. I'd have to create my own computer games because I couldn't afford to buy them." When Mark was sixteen, he got his first taste of teaching computing at a local community centre. Such was his computing skill that Mark was eventually offered a place to read Physics with Computer Science at King's College London, despite his poor grades in other subjects.

To make ends meet, Mark worked at his local DIY store, which is where he had the conversation that was to define his life. "A woman came into the store one day and asked about vacuum cleaners," he recounts. "I explained them to her in such great detail that she complimented me on my explanation. When I mentioned I was doing a degree in Physics and Computer Science she invited me to interview at the tutor agency she ran. Within a month they hooked me up with some tutoring and I never looked back. Nearly twenty years later I'm still tutoring."

Mark ascribes his accomplishments to a number of factors. Firstly, there is his own educational background and the empathy he can offer as a result of that. "A friend of mine is a qualified counsellor and she noticed that the work I do is not far off the kind of work that she does," he says. "Although I am not a trained counsellor I often find myself listening to students and their concerns, understanding where they are coming from and trying to put myself in their position. In fact, *because* I struggled at school, I find it easy to empathise with them. Most of these kids are far better than I was at that age and I make sure to tell them that."

Mark believes that a number of childhood traumas left him with a strong desire to be loved. Unlike many of his peers, he developed an ability to get people to like him quickly, a useful skill that remains with him to this day. But this desire also compelled him to work long hours. He consistently took tedious jobs that other tutors would turn down. "The fact that I never want to go back to the poverty that I saw as a kid has meant I will always work harder than most of my friends who didn't see that," he says. "It is more a subconscious desire and I have to keep it in check or I end up working myself into the ground."

Mark reveals the details of his hectic work schedule. "I worked 8am–10pm every day last week. During the Easter holidays I can easily work for six weeks without a day off, averaging about twelve billable hours a day. I've done well over 18,000 hours of direct one-on-one tutoring in total. It isn't common that people working in education will have that many hours of one-on-one contact." Since the age of eighteen, it's taken Mark nearly twenty years to get to where he is today – a remarkable achievement considering how young he still is.

These working hours aren't just a reflection of how popular Mark is as a tutor, they also have been invaluable for him to learn his trade. "I have no qualifications whatsoever," Mark readily admits. "I did some training at the beginning but it was very basic. I had to teach myself. In some ways I'm glad that I had to teach myself because a lot of the teaching practices that I've seen being implemented are highly ineffective. It's been wonderful to be able to come at it with a clean slate and see what works by trial and error."

Mark believes that it has taken him thousands of hours to become as good as he is. This perspective echoes similar comments made by James Rhodes. The two scenarios might be different but the analogy of decades of hard work to reach that final apex is strikingly similar. Both James and Mark refer to the 10,000-Hour Rule of practise required to attain an elite standard. The 10,000-Hour Rule has effectively become a synonym for the work of psychologist Anders Ericsson. Ericsson's research at Berlin's Academy of Music compares the number of hours practised by the 'best', 'good' and 'least accomplished' student violinists. By the age of twenty, the 'least accomplished' violinists had practised for 4,000 hours, the 'good' violinists for 8,000 hours and the 'best' violinists for 10,000 hours on average. Ericsson went on to compare the results with those of amateur and professional pianists, discovering strikingly similar results. Ericsson's research concludes that once a musician has the ability to get into a top music school, the thing that distinguishes one performer from another is how diligently and how much he or she practised.

Whatever the merits of the 10,000-Hour Rule, the broader benefits of commitment are clear: in both James and Mark's cases, achieving their elite status would not have been possible without the determination and commitment to thousands and thousands of hours to refine their craft.

For Mark, it has made him the sort of tutor who can achieve results very few can replicate, as one particular story vividly emphasises. "I had a seventeen-year-old student a few years ago. He had been kicked out of home at sixteen for drug use and becoming a disruptive person in the family. He went to live in a squat and had effectively alienated himself from his family who were quite wealthy.

"A family friend was an educational psychologist and she managed to get him to agree to complete his A levels. She contacted six tutoring agencies and every one of them ended up calling me. He had a month and a half before his exams, had done no work and had effectively failed his first year A level examinations so was in a particularly tough position. It seemed at best he could possibly scrape some Ds but it was a pretty dire state. It was a salvage job.

"I started by getting to know him as a person, to find out what he was passionate about and what got him excited. I worked hard to understand what had led him to this position in his life and shared some of my own experiences. Eventually he started to see the benefits that hard work could have for his own life, and in achieving what he desired, not just what his parents wanted from him.

"We started with his photography course. I encouraged him to go take some photographs of the things he loved, and I then offered him genuine feedback. He could see that my feedback wasn't just me just trying to be nice. Then I did the same thing with his other work and got him to eventually do his essays. I would often arrive at his house at eight in the morning and ring the doorbell until he got up and stay until he went to bed at night. For a month and a half he and I spent seven days a week together and it was probably one of the toughest assignments I've ever had. Although he was a wonderful boy he had a self-destructive streak, one that I recognised from my younger self.

"After the exams, he went away to Africa for the summer and he came back for his results in August. I was the first person he phoned to tell that he had pulled it off! All As and Bs! Both of us ended up in tears on the phone. He hadn't just turned his life around, he had also changed the perspective his parents had of him. He was back in the household and started to become the master of his own life."

*   *   *

"I suppose my journey starts when I was in care as a kid," **Kevin Godlington** remembers. "I was born with an abominable set of parents – my dad was a career criminal and addicted to heroin for most of his life. So I found myself in children's homes and, as a result of that, I was exposed to a lot of predators in the North of England sink estates and found myself being badly abused.

"I became a delinquent intent on constructing an evil criminal network around me. At sixteen, after a number of brushes with the law and being sternly told I'd end up in prison, I decided to bugger off and join the army, which was probably the most sensible thing for me and for Preston."

If Mark Maclaine typifies the first form of *grit*, to refine one's craft, the second – determination in the face of adversity – is perfectly illustrated by Kevin Godlington. Kevin's start in life was laden with adversity but joining the army was only the beginning for him. "I did one of those entrance exams and they told me I could do pretty much any trade in the British Army, non-commissioned. The highest paying job at the time was surveyor engineer but I quickly worked out I didn't like surveyor engineering because it was boring. I wanted to be a Paratrooper so I did that instead."

Paratrooping was just the beginning for Kevin. "I wanted to join the SAS and be a helicopter pilot, neither of which my bosses thought I'd suit." The doubters ignited Kevin's determination further. "I tend to respond well to people saying you can't do things," he says. "Of course, they were all wrong as I ended up getting into the SAS and I am also now a helicopter pilot."

Since leaving the army, Kevin has gone on to found his own development company specialising in conflict and former conflict nations. He leads investment teams to establish large-scale business in countries which were previously war zones. Kevin's businesses aim to reduce poverty and refocus people's minds away from conflict and towards jobs and future opportunities. Today, he has projects in Ghana, Liberia, Namibia, Afghanistan, Sierra Leone and Somalia and manages assets worth over $100 million.

One example is an organic palm oil business in West Africa. It provides workers with a living wage of $5 a day which can then feed a family of ten dependents. Kevin realized that palm oil was one of the most consumed edible oils in the world, but it could no longer be grown in Malaysia or Brazil so he pursued his own project in Africa. "I figured that there must be a way to grow sustainable, organic oil which didn't kill orangutans or displace people and gave people a living wage. I set about trying to tell the City financiers that this was a good idea. Naturally, they mocked me but, fortunately, I had a few quid myself because I'd sold a couple of businesses already and so I stuck $1 million into it myself." Following the eventual success of the palm oil business Kevin has continued to reinvest the proceeds into agriculture projects such as a teak and eucalyptus forestry projects and even a pineapple plantation.

Arguably, Kevin's most important project is the Network for Children in Need Orphanage, based just outside Freetown, the capital of Sierra Leone. The orphanage has its food, water and education provided by the Godlington Foundation. "I had worked in Africa in the military and knew it well," he says. "I found the poverty in Sierra Leone appalling and it irritated me so much I now run my own orphanage. In Africa, I apply a self-taxation of about ten per cent – a type of Victorian style philanthropic bounty. I have a number of different projects in Sierra Leone, including a hospital and a hydroelectric plant. We employ about 1,000 people in total."

On top of all of this, Kevin is an ambassador for several military charities, he is the founder of the UK's first voluntary social development programme for 15–17-year-olds called the National Citizens Service and he acts as a special advisor to the Prime Minister on youth intervention.

His remarkable career is a long way from sleeping rough in Preston and a vivid example of persistence in the face of damning odds. But what is the hardest thing he has ever done? "I've been shot and that was very unpleasant. Once I walked the entire coast of Sierra Leone from Liberia, living off the land, and got typhoid and malaria for my troubles and nearly died from them. I've done stuff in mountaineering and adventure racing that has been really hard. I've had friends die. They're all hard but I can't isolate a single event. I find it fascinating how people manage to tell you how hard their life is and how hard they toil to be a success. Half the time it's rubbish."

Time and again, Kevin's life is punctuated with 'back to the wall' episodes and that's excluding his classified Special Forces career. There's *grit* behind everything he does. Certainly, to escape the situation he was presented with as a child in Preston takes a fierce and intense resolve. "I always remember wanting to escape from Preston. I knew it was killing me. I was addicted to solvents, was an alcoholic and didn't eat.

"I suppose I always knew that everybody around me was killing me and themselves so I had to get out. It was obvious. I often look at people in similar situations and it still doesn't dawn on them that it's all wrong, that their surroundings are wrong. I don't know whether it's because I was a bit brighter or because I was born with a gift or because I was just lucky, but I knew that I needed to get out of that situation. So joining the army was, for me, the obvious solution."

It remains painfully clear to Kevin what would have happened if he hadn't extracted himself. "My family, sadly, is still in complete disarray. My sister is in and out of prison all the time. She started breeding at fourteen and her four kids are in care. It's a heartbreaking situation but you can't break the cycle. The only reason the cycle was broken for me was by me joining the army. I'm not naïve enough to say that I was born and gifted with a phenomenal ability to drive my way out of these things. The truth is there is no safety net for people like us. If you fall it hurts and you hit the tarmac hard."

*   *   *

The next illustration of *grit* is the determination and drive to pursue every opportunity. **George Bullard** is an explorer, expedition leader and world record holder. In stark contrast to Kevin Godlington, he grew up surrounded by a supportive family and was equipped with an education from one of the finest schools in the world. Despite the absence of adversity in his life, George also exhibits intense grit and determination.

In 2008, at the age of just nineteen, Bullard embarked on an expedition with Alex Hibbert to break the world record for the longest unsupported journey across Antarctica. After 113 days of hauling 200 kilos of equipment and supplies the duo managed to cover 1,374 miles to set a new world record. Despite his relatively young age of twenty-six, he has been pushing the limits of human endurance for over a decade. One of his most recent challenges was to cycle 2,500 miles from London to Greece. In total, he has led expeditions to six of the seven continents of the world; from the depths of the Amazon rainforest to the mountains and plateaus of the Indian subcontinent.

"I have had a few opportunities that most people would have said 'no' to for fear of risking too much," he says, "but I always thought that I had absolutely nothing to lose. You have to be willing to say 'yes' to opportunities that come your way because they may never ever come back. I guess my perception of risk is a bit different. When I see an opportunity that I know will not come round again, it is very difficult to not go ahead and take it."

The first of these opportunities emerged when George was fifteen. "I was given the opportunity by my swimming coach to swim the English Channel. It was a tough selection process and I initially didn't make the cut. I got down to the final round but I was ditched. Even though I was good at swimming long distance in the pool, the cold water got to me when we went to train down in Dover Harbour."

George was hugely disappointed, especially with the cut-off point being so close to the final swim. "I got to the final stages and got rejected the week before the team were going. The swim team were leaving at two in the morning so, while my boarding school housemaster was fast asleep, I snuck out to wave them off. I was so upset to be missing out. But then Nick Adams, the swimming coach, turned to me and said: 'One of

the team is no longer available, do you want to take his place?'
So I ran back into the house and gathered up whatever I needed
and I was off."

Swimming the Channel would prove to be the first of several
long distance challenges that George and his teammates would
attempt. For the next four years, the team didn't think small,
with subsequent swims around New York, Barbados and Lake
Zurich. Again, all of the swims and training required a huge
commitment. "We were training in Dover Harbour early in the
morning and we always sacrificed our Sunday afternoons, the
most prized time of any boarding school child. An incompre-
hensible thing to do."

Nonetheless, the first two swims ended in failure. "We failed
to swim around New York because of the weather," he says. "It
was a race and we were winning and I was just about to get in
and swim past the major sewerage works along the Hudson
River in Manhattan. We were less than 10 kilometres from the
finish of the 50 kilometre course and then there was a tropical
thunderstorm so the race was abandoned. One of my regrets is
that we never asked the boat driver if we could get in and swim
the rest anyway. We had gone such a long way and had sacrificed so much."

This failure, rather than leading to doubt, served to
strengthen the resolve of the team further. "By the next year we
had all learnt from the experience, and the Barbados course was
double the length at 100 kilometres and with sharks and lethal
Portuguese Man of War jellyfish." Once again, the team were
beaten by the elements: "We failed because of the weather. We
were about to get to the major turning point around Barbados
when we had to call if off."

George's positive response to failing is striking. "We did fail
but I am not afraid to stand up in front of an audience and
admit it. It's not a big deal because we did something with it –
the next one in Lake Zurich was successful. That was two of us

swimming a marathon swim of about 25 kilometres together and it was a relatively easy swim in a lake that was warm and it was fun. It was satisfying to finish my last year [at school] on a high."

George's determination has turned disappointment into success on subsequent occasions. With the end of school fast approaching, George applied to read Medicine at university but wasn't offered a place. "I did all the required work experience in care homes, hospices and with surgeons. You name it, I did it. I thought I was a dead cert and would stroll in. All my seven university choices turned me down so I was stuck with another massive failure to add to the list." But the setback ended up giving George the opportunity to take a year out. He joined a British Exploring Society trip to South Georgia and Antarctica, which would prove to be the start of an expeditionary career that has seen him lead groups to six of the seven continents of the world.

Following the trip to South Georgia, George returned to London to give a presentation about the expedition to the Royal Geographical Society. "I walked out of the room and was confronted by a guy called Alex Hibbert who said he had heard all about me. He then offered me an opportunity that changed my life forever. He asked me if I wanted to come with him and break the world record for the longest fully unsupported polar journey. Naturally I didn't want to miss the opportunity and accepted. Alex was mentally determined to do it and had spent two years planning the expedition. He is a hard core ex-Marine. Alex asking me was not only a huge privilege but implied a huge amount of trust because, in the Arctic, we would have to rely on each other to survive."

Trust aside, the challenge itself was staggering – 1,374 miles in 113 days on the ice – and that was without taking into account George's lack of experience. The second time George met up with his fellow explorer was to pack their expedition sledges. Their third meeting took place at Stansted airport, to check-in their bags and fly out to Greenland and start the expedition. "I was scared and apprehensive when the helicopter dropped us on the ice cap. I had never walked on a glacier before nor pulled a sledge so heavy (200kg) nor ever done cross-country skiing. Both Alex and I were apprehensive."

But the mental challenge was just as daunting as the physical. "The physical challenge compared to the mental challenge is nothing. People say they are bored at work but try spending 113 days looking at nothing but endless white. There is no contrast and you don't know how far you can even see. It's so disorientating and extreme boredom sets in."

Meanwhile, George's *grit* was tested to the limit. "After two weeks on the ice we were madly looking for excuses not to be there," he says. The daily grind of pulling a 200kg sledge for eleven hours a day was draining. "That's eleven hours of solid walking every day. I could look back behind me and almost see where we had camped the night before. Mentally that kills you. The weather was miserable and that influences your mood as well. I started to drop back because I was unhappy and trying to get my own personal space, which is ironic because you are in the middle of nowhere. But you can't do that as my partner is so reliant on me for survival and I on him. If a polar bear came along, for example, he was the one that had the rifle. I just started crying into my goggles. The thing that kept me going was not the fear of failure but the fear of missing the opportunity."

George, Kevin and Mark have each carved distinct paths from divergent backgrounds but all of them have shown a remarkable degree of *grit*, whether putting in thousands of hours of tutoring, walking hundreds of miles across icecaps or becoming a Special Forces member. Equally, all have shown a drive to seize opportunities when they arise. Strikingly, all of them have led accomplished lives despite not excelling in their younger years, particularly academically. Their early shortcomings were never perceived as definitive and their *grit* and persistence allowed them to make progress. These *Great Britons* confirm that, by focusing and persisting with a *passion*, not being deterred by setbacks and focusing on long-term ambitions, *grit* can be cultivated to transform one's life.

Chapter 3

Case Study: Lauren Cuthbertson

"The hard work, the graft – that never changes. The discipline and the small technical things are crucial, they keep the cogs turning and facilitate everything."

Lauren Cuthbertson is acutely aware that discipline and hard work are requisites to get to the top. She is a Principal dancer with the Royal Ballet – the highest rank at the Royal Ballet – marking Lauren as one of the leading dancers in the world. She became a Principal in 2008, the youngest ever, at just twenty-three. Since then, she has performed some of the most iconic roles in ballet, including Juliet, Manon, Aurora (*The Sleeping Beauty*) Giselle and Odette/Odile (*Swan Lake*).

Yet, for all her success, her feet remain firmly on the ground, not least because of the dancer's daily routine of stitching her own shoes. "All of our shoes are given to us," Lauren describes during a break in practice at the Royal Opera House in Covent Garden. "We have a pigeon-hole at work. We are given all of our shoes but you have to spend the time to darn them, stitch the ribbons and do the elastics. I go through a pair nearly every day. When doing these things, it reminds me to keep my discipline. When you get to a certain level it's so easy to suddenly relax.

"Yes – it's an absolute bitch to keep stitching all the time but there's something humbling about it as well. It's like life: the truest things are the simplest things and sometimes they are the hardest things. To calmly channel your energies into something that you believe in, and stay true to that, is often the thing that keeps you internally satisfied."

Lauren's journey to become a Principal dancer began in the West Country at a young age. "I started as a tomboy in Devon – a disobedient and hyperactive child. My parents were Scousers who met in Torquay and stayed down there. So, even though I was brought up in Devon and moved to London when I was eleven, I have that temperamental northern soul and I got sent to ballet because my mum had heard of a strict teacher there. I must have been a natural because I won my first competition. I went on to the Royal Ballet School's Associate Programme which nurtures students between the ages of eight to fifteen years old. It meant I had to travel to the beautiful city of Bath each month for training."

But as attractive as the setting was, Lauren didn't enjoy the lessons at first. "I'd been free-spirited up till then – dancing, being expressive and never being too tame," she says. "But when I started the Junior Associate Programme I felt I couldn't breathe. I'd be messing around and didn't have the right discipline or approach and it took me a long time to fall in love with the discipline, the structure and the technique. For me, it was all about the spirit and the story telling."

The discipline to dance wasn't the only challenge Lauren faced as, at the age of just eight, she was forced to focus exclusively on becoming a ballerina. Everything else that Lauren had been involved in, including jazz and Highland and Scottish dance, she had to give up. Even her beloved gymnastics had to be sacrificed because of the crucial postural differences to ballet. "I gave up all the other things and concentrated on ballet. Then, aged ten, I auditioned for the Royal Ballet School and got accepted. They auditioned close to 1,000 girls for a class of just twenty."

As with her time on the Associate Programme, there was a shift in discipline and focus needed for Lauren to succeed. "I was definitely not a fully formed dancer when I arrived. I was awful. I got to go to the school but had quite a bit of trouble fitting in balletically because I was a bit scatty and had a concentration issue. By the second year it finally dawned on me what I had to do to concentrate and there was a massive switch in my mentality.

"When I was training as a youngster I wasn't aware that there were companies across the world that housed different dancers from all over the world and that they did different repertoires. I just wanted to be the next Margot Fonteyn and didn't know anything. I used to fall asleep during ballets and found them so boring. I mean, where was the singing? It was something completely different. From eleven until sixteen proved to be my most formative years where my mind opened up and I realised what I had to do."

There are no shortcuts to becoming a professional ballerina. "Without technique, you can't actually go anywhere. It's pointless. It's like an artist painting with paints that he hasn't mixed well. However naturally talented you are, application and practise are every bit as important." The training routine at the Royal Ballet's Lower School – White Lodge in Richmond Park – was unforgiving. "It was all-consuming. We started class at 8.30am and would work until 6.30pm. Then there would often be choreographic events afterwards or, if not, I would have to stitch up my shoes for the next day – something I'm still doing!

"I had a couple of incredible coaches at school. One of them was Russian and he was actually the boys' teacher, but he would train me during lunchtime – I don't know what it was about me but I could take the discipline and the beating normally reserved for the boys."

After the Lower School in Richmond Park, Lauren was accepted to the Royal Ballet's Upper School in Covent Garden, along with only nine of her year group. Once again, the intensity of competition ratcheted up. "You're suddenly joined by the international students who have been exposed to more international competitions and different ways of training.

YouTube wasn't around so I only learnt about other techniques when I got to Upper School and saw these girls doing it. When I saw a Japanese girl who could spin like a top and a French girl with her extensions I realised there was serious work to do. So I worked on my weaknesses for that whole year."

Lauren describes her time at Upper School as, "intense, endless and physical work" and often reflects on her time there. "It was tough and competitive. Luckily, when you're young, it's painful in a different way because your body is so much more supple. But now my muscles don't recover as quickly. Back then, you could get up every day and just beat the hell out of yourself."

All this hard work was to pay off as Lauren graduated to the company and was then promoted to Soloist in 2002, First Soloist in 2006 and Principal in 2008 – one of only seven.

Lauren's *grit* and determination shone through when faced with injury and illness. The latter came in the form of post viral fatigue syndrome and was so bad that Lauren was in bed for six months and lost her vision.

"I'd wake up every day and the bed would be completely soaking with sweat. I would try to train but would fall asleep at the side of the room instead. I was really sick. But I found an amazing specialist and he helped me. When I went to him I was distraught at what had happened to my career. I was a new Principal of the Royal Ballet, the only British one, and had so much ambition and drive but my illness felt like a sort of thick fog throughout all of my muscles, eyes and brain. I spent six months in bed and, eventually, built myself up to be able to complete a twenty-minute walk. I had to be disciplined and re-teach my body structure."

Compared to the extraordinary amount of practise Lauren was used to, the excruciatingly slow recovery was a shock. It was one thing for Lauren to rebuild her physical strength but it was another to return to her full ballet strength. Not only had she been out for so long but the virus had attacked her hips and meant it would take nine months before she could lift her legs up again. In the end, it took a total of twenty-four months until she was back properly.

Remarkably, the illness wasn't the only major setback to her career as a serious foot injury also took its toll.

"I had noticed some pain and I'd been seeing the physio daily for it but my ankle kept coming forward," she says. "I had one cortisone injection and it lasted for a while. Then I had another injection and then I had two in one go. But I still couldn't dance properly so I went to see the surgeon who found a spur the size of a shark's tooth causing constant inflammation.

"So they took out this chipped bone only to find out, six months later, that I'd actually had spurs and calcifications all across my ankle joints. And then, because the initial surgery had been poor, I had what they called a 'tumour-worth' of scar tissue wrapped around a tendon and not allowing it to move."

The solution became more complicated and involved three surgical procedures. "I eventually saw a Cuban surgeon who had treated the great Cuban dancer Carlos Acosta and whose wife and daughter were also Principal dancers, so he had an understanding of what a dancer needs in their feet and what they don't. After two hours of surgery, they managed to fix it. The surgeon couldn't understand how I had even been able to walk before the surgery."

In total, it took Lauren nineteen months to recover and, on top of the two years to return to full fitness from post viral fatigue syndrome, she spent over three and half years in recovery.

While audiences might watch Lauren perform in a ballet and be amazed at her grace, elegance and beauty, her career has been almost swanlike in its nature: serene and apparently effortless above the surface, but with real strength and determination underneath driving her on.

Trait 3
COMPETITIVENESS

Chapter 1

Case Study: AP McCoy

"I was born in the middle of nowhere. I've got four sisters and one brother and neither my mum nor dad had ever ridden a horse before. My dad was a carpenter by trade and had a bit of land at home so decided to buy a horse to breed from and then became friendly with a local racehorse trainer. From about the age of eight or ten I decided I wanted to be a jockey. It wasn't like I was brought up in racing towns like Newmarket, Lambourn or Curragh – I was brought up nowhere near horses."

The fact that Anthony (AP) McCoy became a jockey at all is something of an achievement. That he rose to become the most successful jump jockey of all time is even more remarkable. He set the unprecedented record of being Champion Jockey in every single year of his illustrious career – twenty consecutive seasons – despite breaking almost every major bone in his body along the way. In 2002, McCoy set the record for most wins in a season with 289, beating Sir Gordon Richards' long-standing record of 269. In 2003, he surpassed Richard Dunwoody's record of 1,699 wins to become the most successful jump jockey of all time. In 2013, he reached the unprecedented milestone of 4,000 wins. To put that into context, only one other jockey in history has ever won more than 3,000 races.

Over the course of his career, McCoy has won all of the most prestigious races in the National Hunt season including the Gold Cup, Champion Hurdle, Champion Chase, King George VI Chase and Grand National. In 2010, he was voted BBC Sports Personality of the Year, the first jockey to ever win the award. He retired in April 2015 having amassed more than

4,300 wins during his career. Indeed, many argue McCoy's achievement will never be repeated.

So what made AP McCoy such a success? Champion trainer Martin Pipe described him as "the best we have ever seen with such a dedication to winning … he would never admit defeat."

McCoy is in a constant competition with himself, let alone his peers. "You have to beat yourself, otherwise you end up like everyone else and float through life," he says. "That is something that has grown in me over the years as I have been lucky enough to be successful. I always feel I have to challenge myself. I can never be as good as I want to be. I can't ever catch what I'm chasing."

When McCoy started his career in Ireland, his relative lack of success didn't seem to dent his ambition or belief. "I started off as an apprentice jockey in Ireland for four and a half years. I wasn't very successful but I always believed, in my heart, something was going to happen."

After a slow start, McCoy's career took off. "It took a long time for it to happen, then, when it did, it all happened quickly. I came to England in August of 1994 and, by the end of the following April, I was Champion Apprentice Jockey and I'd ridden seventy-four winners. I'd had more winners than I'd had rides in the four and a half years before in Ireland."

McCoy always looked for role models to emulate. "When I was starting off as a kid I always looked at who was at the top and why they were the most successful," he says. "When I came onto the scene, Peter Scudamore and John Francome had retired. Richard Dunwoody was the best jockey at the time and I looked up to him but also wanted to beat him and be better."

Winning then became an intense addiction. "The more it happens, the more it becomes an obsession," he explains. "It becomes about numbers. When I was riding winners, especially when I was at [trainer Martin] Pipe's, I felt like it was a factory and I was a robot. Every day I felt it was my divine right to win. Obviously I'm lucky enough to have won a couple of Gold Cups, the Grand National and the Champion Hurdles a few times, but being Champion Jockey and winning the most races overall is much more important to me than winning any of those particular races."

In conjunction with McCoy's intense *competitiveness* is the central idea of competing with himself. He keeps going forward whatever happens and doesn't recognise any limits.

The perfect illustration of McCoy's limitless mindset is his extraordinary ability to tolerate excruciating pain. Over the course of his career he has broken his cheekbone, collarbones, shoulder blades, arms, wrist, thumb, leg, ankle, multiple vertebrae in his back and multiple ribs on multiple occasions. He has also suffered numerous haematomas, punctured lungs and chipped teeth. His familiarity with injury even makes him able to diagnose himself. After a heavy fall in 2013, he diagnosed himself in the ambulance on the way to the hospital. "I knew I had punctured my lung because I couldn't breathe and my sternum was clearly in bits because it was still sticking out. I also knew I had definitely broken my ribs because I'd broken seven or eight ribs and punctured my lung about a year earlier and the symptoms were the same. I know the difference between the pain of breaking something and the pain of being sore. That's just something that comes through experience."

McCoy's competitive streak extends to injury recovery times. "I've been in hospital with broken bones and I would challenge myself to get out quicker than everyone else." Perhaps his most significant injury occurred when he broke his T9 and T12 vertebrae. "I was meant to be in a body cast for three months and I begged the surgeon to operate on me instead." McCoy was so determined to recover in less than eight weeks to return in time for the Cheltenham Festival, the most important and prestigious week of the year for any jump jockey, that he forced the doctor to operate and fuse his vertebrae rather than have months of recovery on a spinal board. After the operation he even aided his recovery by using a cryogenic chamber. Against all the odds, he made it to Cheltenham just in time. "I was back on a horse seven and a half weeks later, and that's just pure power of the mind. If I was listening to the doctor or listening to anyone I wouldn't have been back for months."

For any jockey, injuries are the violent side-effect of competing. "I know that I'm eventually going to end up in the back of an ambulance; that's just the way it is. For the last twenty years I've ridden between 800 and 1,000 horses every year. I don't try and gloss over it but a lot of the time I'll be riding and think I'm invincible. When I do end up in hospital I just think I was unlucky that one time. I convince myself it won't happen again but, in reality, I know that I'm going to end up in hospital."

The most likely explanation as to why McCoy is able to endure such horrific pain on a regular basis is because he is doing a job he truly loves. "No matter what you do in life, if you want to be continually successful you have to really enjoy it," he says. "It has to be your *passion*. It's not meant to be work. You get people like Bill Gates that are already so wealthy and you ask why are they still doing it? Simple – they enjoy it. I think to be continually successful at anything in life you have to enjoy it. I've genuinely never done a day's work in my life."

Competitiveness and *passion* aren't the only factors behind AP McCoy's success; his colossal work rate is another. As he says, "You have to believe in your ability but, to be continually successful, you have to be prepared to work harder than anyone else. I believe that I have the talent to work harder than anyone else."

It's telling that, while McCoy might have had more winners than any other rider, he didn't consider himself the most naturally gifted. "There are probably a lot more natural horsemen than me," he admits, "but when I go out on a horse do I think that they can get from one point to another faster than I can? No."

Importantly, the role of a teacher or mentor was crucial in his development. For McCoy, that figure was the Irish racehorse trainer Jim Bolger. Just as James Rhodes described his piano teacher "in [his] opinion as, aggressive, humiliating, and horrifically critical about everything" but who was instrumental in his success, so McCoy has similar mixed feelings towards Bolger. "I was with him for four and a half years," he says. "I hated every minute of it but it was the best thing that ever happened to me. It was the making of me and made me as mentally tough as I am. Jim Bolger was a perfectionist and he wanted everything done better than everyone else."

To achieve his unprecedented level of success, selfishness has been a close companion to his *competitiveness*. "From age twenty-two to thirty-two, I didn't know what was going on in the world," he admits. "In a very selfish way, it was all about me. I was in my own little bubble. Now, I always stop and give autographs and smile for pictures but between twenty-two and thirty-two I'm not sure I did that a lot. I didn't see anyone at the races; I didn't know or care what was going on around me. As far as I was concerned they were in my way. I was like a robot going around not caring what other people's problems were."

The more success McCoy enjoyed the more he was burdened with a haunting desire to sustain it. "Sometimes I wish I could turn it off or take two months off. I've never been able to do that and switch off. I often wish that I could sometimes be complacent."

By the end of his career he not only wanted to win but he wanted his records to stand the test of time. "I am a statistics person," he explains. "You can't dispute them. When I'm long gone there will be people who believe they're better jockeys than me but not when they look at the stats. I always want my statistics to be better than they are. That's what kept me going, that's what makes me want to get better and that's what makes me want to win more. If someone is going to win more than me, they're going to go through a horrible lifestyle. Whoever does it, I've made it hell for them."

Chapter 2

Competing With Others

"My dad used to play basketball for Wales and held the Sandhurst 400-metre hurdle record so I automatically assumed that was what I had to do when I was younger. I became very competitive and set very high expectations."

Olympic rower **Tom James** has always been competitive and has won gold in the Men's Coxless Four event at both the Beijing and London games. He is also a World Champion, winning gold at the 2011 World Championships in Slovenia, and was President of the Cambridge University Boat Club where he led his university to victory in 2007 in the famous Oxford and Cambridge Boat Race.

Competing is something intrinsic to who he is and a key trait in his sporting success. "I have done numerous after-dinner talks about motivation and competing," he says. "I break it down into basics. Innately, I think that everybody is competitive. When you train, just being next to somebody is a motivating factor. Even playing table football you get competitive, in its most basic form."

Tom recalls playing sport from an early age. "My dad was in the army and we used to live in Berlin, Germany. I remember having access to every sports facility that was out there. You could go swimming, go to the athletics stadium or play tennis on Thursday evening. There was football and then Cubs and Scouts down in the local area. I always enjoyed sport and it was a big part of my life. When I arrived at the King's School in Chester, age thirteen, the school offered rowing. I was tall and had a bit of a dodgy knee at the time so, instead of making the knee worse and running on it playing football or rugby, I tried rowing. That's where it all began."

But what makes a good rower? "Obviously genetics do help," Tom explains, "People with long levers are tall and have a certain capacity but there is also a technical element to it. Psychologically, I found the technical element interesting. I am quite an analytical person and enjoyed the challenge of thinking through the dynamics of how you could apply yourself to make the boat move quicker."

Although Tom's background and proportions were helpful in terms of getting into rowing, they belie the effort and commitment he put in to become successful. "A typical training day starts at 7.30am. At 8.00am we would go out on the water for a couple of hours. We would then have breakfast and then do a second aerobics session. After lunch there would be a final weights session. It's typically a three-session day and works in a cycle. So every third day you might have a half-day rest and then get one day off every five weeks. On top of that, you are away for up to half a year at training camps so the volume is high."

Tom managed the constant strain of training by focusing on goals. "It is very important that you plan out your motivation because a lot of the sessions are tough," he says. "You are training ninety-nine per cent of the time and only one per cent of the time is spent racing so getting through all that training is key. Your goal is so far away that it doesn't mean anything at the end of the day. You need to plot: when is the next stage of the season? When is the next trial? When is the next ergo training? If it is going well, the next goal comes along and you keep doing it."

For Tom, other people were a motivational factor, not just in terms of impressing them but in terms of beating them. "I am happy to admit that we rowers have egos; part of what you do is about beating other people and proving yourself in a very basic and egotistical way."

Tom's competitive streak is apparent in his description of rowing in the Boat Race. After two failed attempts, the race in his final year at Cambridge proved pivotal. "The Boat Race was more important than all of my races," he says. "Had I lost that race, I think I would have probably stopped rowing. It's slightly sad because the Boat Race is such an awesome event to be a part of. But it's really about the winning and losing."

Tom James, as with AP McCoy, is an example of someone with a desperate urge to win, who will do what it takes to achieve that and will be inhospitable company if they don't. They are classic examples of competitors – self-aware enough to know the sacrifices and selfishness that comes with this level of focus, but happy to accept them as the costs of winning. It's striking that gold medallist Tom subscribes to a philosophy opposed to the pure Olympic spirit which emphasises that taking part is what counts. Nonetheless, without his ethos, Tom would most likely not have been at the top of the podium time and time again.

While *competitiveness* is a vital trait for professional sports people, it can also prove a similar driver off the pitch. **Patrick Veitch**, a professional gambler, is a case in point. He started betting at the age of fifteen and is widely regarded as the professional punter the bookmakers fear the most. In less than ten years he won over £10 million betting on horseracing alone. Such was his success that bookmakers avoided taking his business, leading to Patrick establishing a team of 200 agents to execute his bets. In total, it is estimated that bookmakers lost in excess of £20 million to his team.

Patrick sees *competitiveness* as part of who he is. "The thing about betting is you're constantly competing and getting a result. An athlete may compete seriously only six or eight times a year whereas, when I started betting at the age of fifteen, I was already competing up to six or eight times a day and you get an immediate and definitive result each time – you're either right or you're wrong. It's fulfilling if you have a personality that is very competitive."

The desire to win and beat the bookie has driven Patrick to remarkable success. It has also sustained his commitment to refining his craft. Once again, the 10,000 hours of practise rule features. "I'm certainly a subscriber to that 10,000 hours theory. Admittedly it's an arbitrary number but I comfortably pass the figure of 10,000 hours that you're supposed to need. I'm probably nearer 25,000 hours now."

Patrick's success is not just from putting the hours in but from allocating those hours in the right way. "Effort doesn't always equal reward," he reveals. "In the field of betting, people's time could be better spent trying to develop a successful method or strategy rather than just following the horse that won last time. You have to recognise where the betting market's predictions are wrong and assess the reason why and then you can predict the outcome and take advantage."

Patrick acknowledges he has a unique affinity for statistics and analysing data. "I have that type of brain that can naturally see data or facts and compare them with previous facts and then see what's relevant." His talents were recognised early by Cambridge University where he won a coveted place to study Mathematics at just sixteen years of age. The combination of his natural ability with his desire to compete has proved formidable. He masters his craft by focusing on analysing horse form, probability, handicap ratings, weights, bookmaker odds, jockeys, trainers, racecourses, ground conditions, the draw, breeding and numerous other factors. During his first year at university he was almost entirely focused on gambling and set up a premium rate telephone line providing customers with horse racing tips. By the end of his first year, he was employing staff to answer the numerous telephones so he could devote more time to studying horse form. Unsurprisingly, his attendance in lectures waned and his degree lapsed. "I was utterly engrossed in pursuing my future. I briefly reported back to my parents that it hadn't worked out as they had hoped but I always knew it was all for a good cause."

Constant competition brings the adrenaline rush of winning and the dejection of losing, which poses a constant challenge for self-control. "You're trying to train yourself to feel as little as possible," Patrick explains. "I think of it in terms of a pulse rate. If you were trying to pick a successful gambler, you would measure their heart rate before a race until after the finish. The ones most likely to succeed would be those with the smallest change." This is easier said than done. Weekly losses of £100,000 are common for Patrick. In a matter of days he may lose £150,000. Once, in an unprecedented run of failure, Patrick lost over £400,000 in a matter of weeks. "Many people would become disappointed if they had two very bad days losing money. I learnt to think about things differently. It's like neuro-linguistic programming. You program yourself to think you are not down X pounds over two days but, instead, that you are up Y pounds for the year. If you started badly in January you'd only be thinking how far ahead you were over the last few years – or even the decade – if necessary. Think about it like owning shares in a company: if your shares are up over the last year you tend not to stress out if they go down for two days."

Just as difficult to deal with is coping with winning, which requires a level-headedness and discipline to not get carried away. Patrick has had many purple patches with his most profitable periods sometimes generating around £1.5 million over several weeks. For two consecutive years he won over £2 million and, in one spectacular period of eighteen months, he won nearly £4 million. "There's only so much reflection on recent successes that is useful, so you try to do that enough to spot whether you're doing well but not so much that it's affecting your day," he says. "It's inevitable that you're going to be a little bit more pleased with yourself on a Saturday evening after a very good week but you're trying to minimise that effect if possible. Equally, you can't have a situation where you mentally shut out all the losses but have big euphorias for every win."

Overall, Patrick recognises a competitor must draw on defeat and failure. "The good thing about competition is you get to experience failure on a daily basis," he says. "I've never seen a situation where a competitor goes through a season and wins every race. I get knocked back constantly." The most defining knock back for Patrick occurred one morning in June 1998 when a notorious criminal arrived on his doorstep unannounced and demanded a colossal sum of money – or have both his legs broken. In the days that followed, Patrick, with the help of the police, was forced to go into hiding. He sold his house and car and had no choice but to cut off communication with his family and friends. He became completely anonymous and disappeared for two years to ensure his safety. "It all comes back to 1998," he explains. "I wouldn't have achieved half as much if I hadn't been spurred on by what happened to me that terrifying day in June."

Both Tom and Patrick have achieved their success in the sporting world. Sport is the perfect arena for a competitive type as they are continually being given the opportunity to measure themselves against others and that desire to win is clearly a central motivator.

In both their cases, their love for competing has spurred them on to devote the hours needed to succeed even when, as in Tom's case, he doesn't particularly enjoy that time spent training. They both have clarity in their thinking, showing a self-awareness of their *competitiveness*, which allows them to harness it rather than being controlled by it.

Competing against others is a great form of motivation but, sometimes, the person to compete with can be found closer to home.

Chapter 3

Competing with Yourself

"What I love about the North Pole is that the value in arriving at the North Pole is only that which you ascribe to it. It's entirely conceptual and personal. There is nothing there. It's sea ice. There is no physical pole. There is no grandstand. The BBC isn't there. You don't feel the world spinning. It's just a point that happens to be there.

"At the South Pole, there is a building and a base with flag-poles but the North Pole is purely abstract and I like that aspect of it. Sports are different because there are gold medals you can win at the end of them and they've got cheering grandstands.

"For twenty-five years, I kept looking for something I could do where my particular assortment of skills, interests and attributes, as a package, if properly identified, managed and improved over time, would enable me to excel. It turned out that exploration and adventure involves all of those that I have. You need to understand your physiology, your psychology, technical equipment, navigation, the environment, the spon-sors and the marketing. I love that you can bring everything to it. In a typical job you can't."

Pen Hadow's success and *competitiveness* is different to that of AP McCoy, Tom James or Patrick Veitch. In the world of exploring, you're not racing or measuring yourself against rivals, nor are there fans cheering you on. The only person to worry about and challenge is yourself.

Not only has Pen reached both the North and South Poles but he has done so by trekking without resupply from external parties and by travelling from the continental coastlines of

North America and Antarctica respectively. His North Pole feat has never been repeated since.

To achieve such feats takes a combination of physical and psychological strength. The importance of the latter, in particular, can't be understated. "I would say that eighty-five per cent of the challenge is the management of your psychology in the field and is what determines whether you get to the far end," Pen reveals. "It's not the technical skills, equipment, clothing, rations, fitness, or strength that are key. In the case of the North Pole, it's managing your psychology.

For example, some call the Arctic environment 'hostile' but that is giving it a personality it hasn't got. It's just there. It has no idea you're there. Words like 'hostile' frame it as a fight. Can you slay the proverbial dragon and conquer the Arctic? No. You're not going to *conquer* the Arctic. That is just what journalists write."

So how did Pen motivate himself to reach the Pole? It turns out Pen has been finding ways to push himself from a very early age.

"My mother can remember me sitting on a horse at a fairground merry-go-round and saying to her, 'I'm not interested in this and all these people. This is all very ordinary and I don't want to be ordinary. I want to be extraordinary'. I have always been interested in the interface between the physiological limits of what you're able to do and how that interfaces with your psychology. For example, when I was eight years old I thought it would be interesting to hang myself upside down on an apple tree by my legs and see how long I could do it for. After nearly four hours my head was really swollen and my mother came charging out to get me. She was horrified. It was my own little experiment to see what it would feel like and how long I could do it for."

Pen excelled as a young boy, becoming head boy at all his schools, including the prestigious boys school Harrow. In 1977,

Pen then challenged himself to run the infamous Long Ducker – an endurance run just shy of a marathon from Harrow-on-the-Hill to Marble Arch in London and back again. Despite being in his early teens he completed the endurance run, a feat so demanding that there is no record of it ever having been done before by a Harrow schoolboy.

Pen would continue pushing himself and aiming ever higher. It wasn't just school that fuelled the fire but also Pen's father. Pen comes from a family of high achievers; his great-great-uncle, for example, made the first ascent of the Matterhorn in 1865 and another family member, Frank Hadow, is the only Wimbledon Champion to have never dropped a set on his way to victory (he also introduced the 'lob' to tennis to thwart a master volleyer and win the final). His father, in particular, encouraged him to aim high. "My father used to tell me about my forebears. I sensed that he felt that a couple of generations had been missed out from the good old days when the Hadows really strode the global stage winning Wimbledon and climbing the Matterhorn. I feel that he was preparing me as best he could to realise that these things were possible and you could think big. That you might be surprised how far you can get if you just apply yourself."

With the encouragement to think big, Pen began to plot how to create an impact on the world stage. "I have developed, over time, this system of putting a marker in the ground a long way out in front of where I want to be," he says. "I then work backwards via key milestones to where I am today. Then, I have my plan. That's how I do it."

Psychologically, Pen will think big in terms of the overall goal but then will break it down into smaller components to make that challenge achievable. This seems an imperative strategy when competing against yourself. "When trying to reach the North Pole, I let go of the Pole. I don't think about it. On the first day I will set off, cover some ground and then get the tent up and get some food.

"I think mindset is a choice …
Bad things happen to everyone. It
is completely naïve to think that
you are the only person with
something bad going on. But it is
how you get on with it, that is the
real test of a person's character."

Guy Disney, ex-serviceman
and polar adventurer

Lauren Cuthbertson, principal of the Royal Ballet

Levison Wood,
explorer and author

Jamie McDonald,
adventurer and fundraiser

Eliza Rebeiro,
charity founder

James Rhodes,
pianist and author

Simon Woodroffe,
entrepreneur

Roz Savage, solo
ocean rower and
world record holder

Kirsty Henderson, Shidokan
black belt and world champion

Chrissie Wellington,
Ironman world champion
and world record holder

Mark Maclaine, tutor

Gilo Cardozo, inventor
and engineer

Pen Hadow,
polar explorer

George Bullard, world
record-breaking explorer

Linzi Boyd,
entrepreneur

"From the moment that I woke up
I knew what the surgeons had
done was irreversible and I knew
that burns leave behind an horrific
injury. So, in my mind, there was
no way to go other than forward
because if I dwelt on the injury I
would never get anywhere in life."

Karl Hinett, ex-serviceman
and ultramarathon runner

The next thing is to move day by day and get to the second day, then to the third day. Then, do five days. Five days is good because it's embarrassing to come back after less than that. Initially, the fear of failure, humiliation and embarrassment is an enormous driver for me to keep grinding it out. Then it's day seven and that's the first week done. Then you've done your first ten days. Then fourteen, which is two weeks. Then you do it in multiples of ten, fifteen and twenty so you're never far away from reaching another week or another five-day block.

Finally, you start to count in latitudes as you move from 83 to 84 degrees north. By 87, the Pole is there (at 90 degrees North) and you've got a lock-on, like a fighter pilot, and you can dare to think that you can nail it."

Clearly, setting goals and having targets to aim at are paramount.

Entrepreneur Michael Acton-Smith puts it succinctly: "I like to have big visions. In his book *Good to Great*, Jim Collins called them 'BHAGS' or 'big, hairy, audacious goals'. When in doubt, I like to set myself ridiculous targets."

For many, having sights aimed high is a great motivator but for others their goal-setting is something that develops more organically. **Heather Fell**, a World Champion in the Modern Pentathlon, fits the latter. Modern Pentathlon is a gruelling sport that demands skill in swimming, fencing, horseriding, shooting and running. Heather's glittering career includes two golds and a silver at the Junior World Championships in 2003, European Silver in 2007 and 2009, a gold medal in the 2008 World Cup series, Olympic silver medal in Beijing 2008, and gold in the 2012 World Championships Team.

Incredibly, despite her achievements at the Junior World Championships, Heather originally envisioned going to the Olympics not as an athlete but as a physiotherapist, a subject that she was studying at university. "At university, one of the lecturers mentioned that being a physio at the Olympics in four years' time would be impossible because I wouldn't have the level/experience. So when I eventually realised I wasn't going to get there as a physio, I thought I would try and get there as an athlete."

For Heather, the goals and inspiration for Pentathlon emerged over time as she became more familiar with the sport. "A good season had given me a flavour of what to expect and I began to formulate a goal. I started to realise the calibre of events I was competing in and suddenly getting to the Olympics *was* my goal," she divulges. But her journey was not without its difficulties – her Lottery funding ended and she was hampered by injuries. "The problems I faced actually gave me the goal. Setbacks can actually give you goals because you're no longer able to drift along. In 2006, all my funding ended and that made me realise what I wanted to do and what I wanted to get out of my career."

Interestingly, Heather differs from some of the other *Great Britons* with her more modest goal-setting. "It never was my goal to actually go and win a medal," she admits. "Instead, it was to get into the best competition I could possibly get into and then to perform the best I could. I was never visualising being on a podium." Rather than feeling motivated by having huge goals, Heather finds them restricting and performs better when she is relaxed and exceeding expectations. "I'm more driven when it's motivation from within," she continues, "I push back if people try and push me to do something, which is a bit strange and not ideal in a strict training environment. I think I'd be terrible if I was in the army."

Heather openly admits she was a nightmare to coach as a result. "If I was expected to run a time but I thought it was too fast I would sometimes deliberately be slow just to prove that I was right," she says. "If I'm training on my own I somehow go faster because no one expects me to. I feel relaxed and motivated if I know I can beat the target time. When I'm actually beating my times, I feel better and I run faster, whereas if I'm not making my times I get frustrated. I think setting your own goals is key."

The *Great Britons* in this chapter illustrate how *competitiveness* is a significant driver behind remarkable achievements. For some, like Tom James, it is crushing opponents that typifies *competitiveness* while for others, like Pen Hadow, it is about competing against himself.

Goal-setting is a great way to motivate and compete but different types of goals will benefit different types of people. Michael Acton-Smith aims for 'big, hairy, audacious goals' while Heather Fell's beatable targets are at different ends of the same spectrum. The results are an overriding desire to compete.

While *competitiveness* in the world of sport is expected, this trait is evident across the *Great Britons* and across diverse fields; from Michael Acton-Smith in business to James Rhodes at the piano or Lauren Cuthbertson on the stage, all of them are competing with others, or sparring with themselves on their path to achieving remarkable feats.

Chapter 4

Case Study: Chrissie Wellington

"Even as a primary school child I was competitive with myself and everybody else. I was very hard on myself and self-critical. I'd set myself rules and, if I didn't abide by them, I'd chastise myself. For example, I hated it if my dad or mum swore. It would create anger and real frustration in me if I swore or heard someone else swear. Now I'm older, I've learnt to not be so judgemental."

Chrissie Wellington is no ordinary athlete. She is a professional triathlete and four times World Champion in Ironman Triathlon. The Ironman Triathlon is the single toughest one day endurance event for any athlete. Contestants have to complete a 2.4 mile swim, then a 112 mile bike ride and finally run a full 26.2 mile marathon to finish. Over the course of her career Chrissie has dominated the women's Ironman competition by setting the world record, achieving the four fastest times ever recorded and the greatest number of sub-nine hour finishes. Remarkably, Chrissie was undefeated in all her Ironman races.

To complete an Ironman Triathlon takes great courage and determination but to compete at the elite level Chrissie has reached is rare. Unsurprisingly, her motivation touches on familiar themes including the encouragement of competition, both with others and yourself, and specific goal-setting.

Chrissie breaks her success down into three key elements. The first is *passion*. "I think the most important thing to achieve success in anything is to make it a passion," she says. "But, first of all, you need to go back one step further and actually know

92

what your passion is. So many people bumble through life not knowing what they're passionate about and don't actually consider what makes them happy, what makes them smile or laugh or really puts a firework up their backside. It's important that people go through that process of self-reflection. Then, when you have that passion, it makes it a lot easier to set a goal.

"Setting a goal is the second step and there are different approaches. You must make it ambitious but not unrealistic. If you've never run before, it would be unrealistic to set a goal of running across Africa. It's a more realistic goal if you say you want to do it within two years or if you want to run a marathon within six months. It's about making it challenging but achievable.

"The third step is to build incremental steps towards your 'A' goal. Unless you identify those intermediary steps, or 'B' goals, you forget to celebrate any progress. In sport, for example, my 'A' goal was the Ironman World Championships. I had my 'B' races – other Ironman races and half-Ironman races which weren't as important but I still prepared for them.

"Each of those was a stepping stone for me to assess, test and celebrate my progress along with the daily training sessions. You've got to have those intermediary goals, otherwise you're so focused on the final outcome that you forget to look at how far you've come."

In some ways, her split between 'A' and 'B' goals is a combination of the different approaches of Michael Acton-Smith or Heather Fell. Expanding on the subject of goals, Chrissie mentions the influence of renowned sprinter Michael Johnson's book *Slaying the Dragon* on her thinking.

"[Johnson] is a unique individual and his focus was on winning the 200 metres *and* the 400 metres," she says. "He believed he could do it. In every race he went into, he believed he could win. I was different. I didn't go into every race or every event with the goal of winning, although I then did, so our approaches were slightly different. Like Michael Johnson, I have this desire and compulsion to do the very best I can at whatever I'm doing at any point in time.

"That's always been my goal, so what I've done is underestimate my potential, as it were. That's what has enabled me to be successful. Unlike Michael Johnson, I didn't have the goal of winning every race I did. My goal was to finish the race. What you should never lose sight of is the desire to do your best at any one moment in time, being able to follow a plan, being able to adapt and being open to that goal being possible."

This echoes Heather Fell's approach of not thinking about the podium. Perhaps, like Heather, Chrissie achieved by not overloading herself with pressure. "The next characteristic or strategy for success is the ability to plan, and to set a programme based on your overall goal; to set and follow a plan requires help from everyone else. It requires discipline, dedication, motivation and, most importantly, consistency. There is no point in having a great three days if you have to spend the next four days of the week knackered or unable to get out of bed. You've got to have consistent training all the way through."

Chrissie talks about things getting tough and she means it. The amount of training required to compete at an elite level means that being able to motivate yourself is of paramount importance.

"I'm always asked how many hours a week I train, and it's twenty-four hours a day, seven days a week. As a professional athlete, you have to take absolute care of the minutiae. For me, that means training 24/7. That means swimming, biking and running sessions of about thirty hours a week. Then strength and conditioning, then rest and recovery, then sleep, massage, physiotherapy, shopping for food and making sure my nutrition is right. If you don't take care of the minutiae in any job that you're in or anything you're trying to do you won't reach the pinnacle."

Chrissie is always trying to find that little bit extra to give her an edge against her competitors. "There are only so many ways to skin a Triathlon cat and, when I lived and trained with everyone in Boulder, Colorado, we all knew what we were all doing," she says, "but the difference was the time that was spent on taking care of the other things: your nutrition, your sleep or getting the best massage therapist. I'm always amazed by the number of athletes that focus on the sessions that they've done but fail to tell me how many hours sleep they've had a night. As amateur athletes, they might be training two or three hours a day but if they only sleep four hours a night they are undoing a lot of the work. It's the recovery that enables you to benefit from the training."

For all the physical element of training, Chrissie knows that the mental aspect is just as important. "Physical training means you put stress on your body," she explains. "Recovery is what enables you to strengthen yourself from that stress. Part of that process is training the brain. Getting your body in shape is only half the battle. Getting your mind in the right frame to be able to succeed is another and I think that is the undoing for many people. A lot of people are physically talented but they don't have the psychological attributes necessary to be successful. They're not training their brains. There are strategies that you can adopt to train your mind to be stronger. Some of those are innate but there are also strategies you can use to make yourself more motivated, more focused or to make you more able to cope with pain and discomfort."

Chrissie stresses the importance of competing with yourself. "Success is a decision and not a gift," she says. "It's a decision that you make to want to excel. We can all accept mediocrity or we can all decide we want to excel in whatever we do, whether it's excelling in being the best friend you possibly can, whether it's brushing your teeth in the best way that you possibly can, doing the washing-up really well, or becoming Ironman World Champion."

95

She mentions the importance of the role that other people can play in your success, both in the shape of your support team and your rivals. "I think it's important to share the journey and that's something that I found hard because I have always been fiercely independent. For me, I'd like to achieve things independently, which doesn't always make me a good team player. What I learnt through sport, especially, is that I needed to rely on other people, even though I was actually racing alone.

"It was difficult for me, especially initially, to lean on others, to ask advice from others and to accept my coach. I think it's only when I started to accept my coach that I started to accept advice from other people. I started to admit when I was tired, when I wasn't feeling good or when I felt I couldn't do something. It was when I started to lean on others and reveal my vulnerabilities to my inner circle that I was then able to achieve more than I could have possibly achieved alone."

Curiously, Chrissie even saw her rivals as an extension of her team. "In a weird way, my competitors are also part of my team," she reveals. "If you look at the Latin root of the word competitor, it means 'to seek together or strive in common'. It's what you're doing as competitors – competing together and 'seeking together' and they enable me to elevate my performance.

"I'm sure, in business, Microsoft has enabled Apple to elevate its performance because they compete. I think it was the same with me. It definitely made me better."

The idea of competition being a shared goal is a compelling insight. In many respects, it sums up what *competitiveness* is about: using the essence of competition as a means to further oneself. Chrissie and her fellow *Great Britons* have successfully channelled this sentiment for their own ends. Whether the goals are big and hairy or realistic and achievable, it's an ethos that anyone can apply to their own lives.

Trait 4

BOLDNESS

Chapter 1

Case Study: Jamie McDonald

"As a kid, I had a condition called syringomyelia, which meant sometimes I couldn't move my legs and I also had immune deficiency and epilepsy. But at nine years old, I started to move my body. I was lucky because I could have lost my mobility or lost my life. By my twenties, I was working as a tennis teacher and I was saving to put a deposit on a house. Then I realised I didn't actually want the house and the only reason I was buying the house was because everyone else was buying one. So, I backed out at the last minute. At that point, I started to think about what I wanted out of life. I started to reflect on what I went through as a kid. Because I wasn't buying the house I decided to do something out of my comfort zone. I wanted to give back to the hospitals that helped me out as a kid and go on an adventure and raise money for them."

Jamie McDonald began his extraordinary globetrotting odyssey of charity events as a result of a childhood afflicted with ailments. He began with a herculean cycle ride, travelling back to his hometown of Gloucester from Bangkok, Thailand. It was a journey that covered 14,000 miles, six time zones and dozens of countries along the way. Two days after arriving home from his mammoth journey Jamie attempted and surpassed the static cycling world record. After more than eleven days he stepped off the bike with a new world record of 268 hours 32 minutes and 44 seconds, beating the old record by more than forty-four hours. In his next challenge, Jamie swapped his pedals for running trainers. In February 2014, he became the first person in history to run 5,000 miles unsupported across Canada from the Atlantic coast to the Pacific Ocean, exhausting thirteen pairs of trainers along the way. To add to the tens of thousands of pounds raised in his earlier challenges, Jamie raised another $250,000 for sick children in Canada and the UK.

Remarkably, Jamie had no background or experience in any of these challenges. "I'd never even cycled before," Jamie admits referring to his Bangkok-Gloucester journey. "I didn't even try out the bicycle beforehand. I just flew to Bangkok and I had no idea what I was doing."

Jamie's adventures are *boldness* personified, deliberately departing his comfort zone without knowing where it would take him. "When I was running across Canada I learnt there are two kinds of people, the 'naïve' and the 'planners'," he says. "The 'planners' can plan up to stage eight or nine, but once they get beyond that, where they can't plan, they decide not to go ahead. But the 'naïve' don't think about stage eight, nine or ten, the naïve just keep plodding through."

Jamie is the latter. "Preparation, to me, is just fear. I avoid all planning and preparation like it's the plague. All it does is put fear in me." It might sound counter-intuitive, but for the size of challenges that Jamie takes on, it is this lack of planning that he feels is integral to his success. Of his journey across Canada, Jamie says, "you can't train for something like that. At what point can you confirm you are fit enough to run across Canada? My training started while I was on the adventure. When you're taking on these big expeditions, you can't plan every day because you don't know what's going to happen."

There is a sense of innocent naïvety in Jamie's approach, but his terminology belies the *boldness* and courage underpinning his approach. Describing the bicycle that took him back to England, Jamie says, "I put it on the plane and assembled it for the first time in Bangkok. I was so excited until a bolt came off the bike and I realised I had no idea how to fix it. I had spares but I didn't know how to use them. When that bolt came off, it suddenly dawned on me what I had got myself into. I found a hotel and puked over the toilet. But then I convinced myself it was going to be okay and I just got cycling. I didn't plan anything so I was always in the moment."

It wasn't just a lack of bicycle maintenance skills that Jamie's journey would suffer from, his laissez-faire attitude also meant he hadn't planned a proper route home. "I didn't take a map. To get out of Bangkok I had to go to the west. All I had was a compass, so I just went for it using random roads."

The same approach was used in Canada as he ran each day not knowing where he was going to sleep that night. "Every day I would run and there would be no expectation whatso-ever," he says. "So every experience that happened was golden, whether finding a toilet or knocking on the door of a house and getting a bed for the night.

"One morning it all went wrong. I had been sleeping rough for days and a family offered me a shower and a bed in their home town which was twenty-five miles away. I took their phone number and by the end of the day I had reached their town. I called the number and it was the wrong number. It was as if my whole world was ripped apart. I'd had the expectation and it didn't materialise. It goes to show that, if there is no expectation, then everything is great."

The *boldness* of Jamie's decision making was clear when he decided to make a detour to visit a children's hospital in Toronto, adding 300 miles to his journey. This was the equiva-lent to another twelve days of running at a time when the weather was against him. "I knew the winter was setting in on the west side of the country," he continues, "but I made the decision to go to the children's hospital anyway because it would help fund-raising go through the roof. It was a hard decision because the detour was jeopardising the whole trip.

"Nonetheless, I stuck a Flash superhero outfit on and convinced myself to go for it. The superhero outfit made me more like the person I wanted to be and soon everyone was giving me high-fives, waving and smiling. It was making everyone happy and it was making me happy. It was a distraction from the suffering of running.

"When I reached the hospital a few kids were dressed as Spider-Man and Iron Man and all the doctors and nurses came out to support. At that point I realised, even if I didn't make it all the way across Canada, no one could take away the experience I'd had, the people I had met, and the money I had raised.

"To give back is one of the most satisfying things anyone can ever do. But it was way more than just about fund-raising. The inspiration of what I was doing touched people and that became my motivation in the end. People would come up to me while I was running and they were so full of emotion some of them would cry. I didn't know how to deal with it at first but then I realised this was actually changing lives. Children's hospitals were the core reason for running and I'm glad that I ended up fund-raising for one children's hospital in every province in Canada."

Throughout Jamie's challenges being told he couldn't do something seemed to act as a spur to push him on. Crossing the Rockies – a distance of about 1,000 miles – saw him running against the advice of the local rangers. "The rangers supported me for a couple of days, even though they hated what I was doing. They said it was impossible and that I was going to die as no one had ever crossed the Rockies at this time."

As Jamie crossed the Rockies he was motivated by messages sent to him via social media. For example, a family, who Jamie had met earlier on his run, had got in touch to say their son was running out of treatment options and his cancer had returned. "That was the moment I realised that I was out there making a

difference," he says. For Jamie, it was the taking part and not the winning that counted.

It seems attempting these challenges is instinctual for Jamie and, perhaps, is why he is so resistant to the planning and preparation. "When I do these adventures, it is like I'm going back 5,000 years ago, when conditions were tough and we were battling for our lives," he says. "As exhausting as it is, I just love it."

Thousands of years ago, a man's life involved being bold and taking risks and pushing yourself beyond normal limits to survive. Jamie, like many of the *Great Britons*, has these ancient traits in abundance.

Chapter 2

Boldness in Actions and Boldness in Ideas

When it comes to *boldness*, the *Great Britons* interviewed manifest the trait of risk taking by two different means. First, there are the risk-takers who thrive outside their comfort zone and embrace physical discomfort. Second, there are those who are bold with their ideas; they adopt an unconventional or innovative path for their business or to achieve their goals. In both forms, the physical and the intellectual, *boldness* can spawn a virtuous circle of self-belief.

Jamie McDonald's audacious cycle ride from Bangkok and 5,000 mile run across Canada typifies both types of *boldness*. The *boldness* to reject a conventional career and the daring to embrace extreme physical hardship and discomfort. His challenges also vividly display the virtuous circle of self-belief as, upon finishing each challenge, he was emboldened to take on the next one.

Someone who knows all about pushing themselves and spending time in their discomfort zone is ocean rower **Roz Savage**. "On my first voyage, when I was on the boat and struggling with the Atlantic rowing, I was so far out of my depth, literally and metaphorically, it wasn't even funny," she describes.

In the first section on *passion*, Roz described writing her own obituaries and facing the choice between a life in her comfort zone or a life in the discomfort zone. Having chosen the latter path, Roz was determined to put herself in situations that challenged her. "My first adventure was when I went to Peru in 2003, the year after my marriage ended and three years after I left my job in the City," she recalls. "It was the first time I'd travelled on my own and I remember being really scared on the plane on the way over there. I had a two-week crash course in Spanish, but I'd never travelled on my own before and this was going to be far outside my comfort zone."

The deliberate decision to place herself in such a situation was repeated in her solo Atlantic row. "Whenever I was asked by a journalist what my motivation was for rowing I would always reply that it was about getting outside of my comfort zone," she says.

Once in the boat, it didn't take long for Roz's discomfort to manifest itself. "My shoulders had tendonitis, I had salt-water sores on my bottom, my sleeping bag was wet and everything was so uncomfortable and miserable," Roz remembers. "But the fact that I was uncomfortable didn't mean that I was failing in some way. It actually meant that I was succeeding in what I set out to do." Roz then managed to turn a difficult situation into something encouraging. "That flipped the discomfort from a negative and into a positive. Since then, I even get uncomfortable if I'm too comfortable, because I feel I'm not pushing myself or learning something new."

For Roz, the discomfort wasn't masochism but had a purpose. "Out on the Atlantic, I realised the harder it was, the more rewarded I felt in the end," she explains. "When you work really hard for something, you know you deserve the reward and that feeling of success at the end."

For Roz, the crossing was hard. "I was overwhelmed by the Atlantic at first," Roz says. "It was a 3,000 mile journey and my electronic chart plotter calculated that, at my rate of progress, it would take me three years to complete the journey. Sometimes, if the current was blowing me backwards, it would even say an infinite number of years, which is completely crushing to morale. So I decided to reconfigure the screen display and remove that data field. It was a psychological game with myself out there."

Roz came up with two particular techniques to win the psychological battle. The first of these was to find a way of creating a sense of progress. "I would write the degrees of latitude or longitude on the whiteboard in front of my rowing seat so I could actually cross them off as I passed them. That gave me a sense of achievement. Having a visual provides a sense of progress, especially because the ocean pretty much looks the same every single day. On land, you have physical landmarks whereas, on the ocean, the landmarks are just little numbers on your GPS. There isn't anything physical to see."

The second technique was developing an understanding that progress can be inconsistent. "The other important thing I realised is that progress is not always linear and, in fact, this applied to business as well as rowing or whatever challenge you are undertaking. You often feel like you are slogging away at something and not making any real progress and then, after months and months of slogging away, the stars suddenly align and there's a burst of progress and positive outcomes."

The discomfort that Roz put herself through on the Atlantic crossing brought its reward when she arrived in the Caribbean. "That feeling when I stepped ashore in Antigua was amazing. It wasn't just the three and a half months on the ocean but, also, the fourteen months of preparation before that. It was entirely my project and I'd given it everything I had. In fact, I gave it more than I even knew I had and it paid off. That feeling is just euphoric."

Beyond the initial thrill of completion, there was something deeper in how the journey affected Roz and one that took her a while to assimilate. "The Atlantic row was three and a half months and, without a doubt, was the most transformative time of my life," she says. "It was such a steep learning curve that I couldn't even keep up with it. I'd have these mini-epiphany moments and write them down in my log book. It took about two years of processing once I got back on dry land. I had to weave what I had learnt back into my ordinary life."

Roz found a way of translating this into her ordinary life by transferring that same feeling of discomfort into the world of business. "My business partner and I are launching a new business and I have no idea what I'm doing," she says. "I'm not a natural entrepreneur so, technically, I'm back to being uncomfortable again. I now know that the 'discomfort zone' is where you do the growing and I've developed an appetite for discomfort and figuring out how to get through challenges. I hope I keep doing that until the end of my life."

For Roz, there is a sense of pride when reflecting on her bold feats. "For me, success is knowing that I did my best against the goals that were important to me," she says. "Some people may argue that I'm a forty-six-year-old who doesn't own her own home or car and doesn't have a pension plan, and question what I have done with my life. But I look at the experiences that I've had, the people I've met, the friendships I have and the ways that I've challenged myself and succeeded against my own criteria, and I feel successful."

Boldness and risk-taking is not confined to rowing across an ocean or walking to the North Pole. As Roz showed by moving into the world of business, you can take yourself out of your comfort zone in any walk of life. As mentioned earlier, the second illustration of the *boldness* trait is associated with ideas. If your ideas are unconventional, non-conformist, innovative or audacious, then there is no reason why you can't be bold without ever having to leave your desk.

John Neill is a good example of someone who has prospered in business as a result of the *boldness* of his actions, ideas and decision making. When he originally became Managing Director at British Leyland Parts, he found himself in the thick of dealing with a crisis from day one and facing an unprecedented union strike costing the business millions of pounds.

"It was a toxic place to work," John remembers, "people weren't happy and the unions were intimidatory. I decided to fix the company my way and get the staff to come back and work hard." His strategy was easier said than done as this was a time in British history when the trade unions were an incredibly powerful body. To take on the unions and win was a seismic event and an upturning of the natural order of the 1970s.

Part of John's strategy was to do something unheard of at the time – to talk directly to the workers. "In those days, management were not allowed to communicate directly with the employees or the whole company would go on strike," he remembers. "To get the employees to come back and work we did innovative things like communicate directly with the employees' families and take full page ads in the newspapers giving people the truth by being unambiguous. They could sign up for it or they could leave." It was a bold strategy but one that proved successful.

John's unconventional thinking was also evident during the economic difficulties of the early 1980s. "The '80s was the worst recession I'd ever experienced in my life," he says. "Interest rates were at twelve per cent, unemployment was high and the economy was in a bad place. Everybody was cutting costs and firing people. I decided that, instead of cutting and running away from the recession like everyone else was doing, we would invest and take market share."

John's bold decision was to establish the first ever commercial marketing division for an industrial company in the UK. "We built a brand, a retail shop programme and a network to introduce new products and make our brand the best known in the country," he explains. John used new communication and persuasion techniques. He increased the advertising budget fivefold and worked with esteemed advertising agency Saatchi

& Saatchi to produce impactful adverts, including the iconic television advert promoting oil filters, an unexciting but highly profitable product for the company. "We got Pat Jennings, the Tottenham Hotspur goalkeeper at the time," he recalls. "He was hugely famous and we dressed him up as an oil filter saving chunks of grime and grit in a goal. The sale of oil filters went up 400 per cent."

John also decided to spend £1 million on a single sentence advertisement – 'The answer is yes – now what's the question?' – "It was probably one of the most memorable ad campaigns in the industry, people still talk about it," he says. "We said to all the consumers that, if you want a vehicle component from us, the answer is yes – now what's the question? We used the advertising to engage people. We destroyed the competition, absolutely destroyed it."

However, John's finest moment would eventually come in 1987 when he led a management buyout to turn Unipart into a private and employee owned company. At the buyout, the company used a three hour theatrical show to explain the risks and opportunities of the employee share ownership scheme. The scheme was massively oversubscribed and has led to thousands of employees profiting from the success of the company. John has now led the company for over thirty years making him the longest serving CEO of any major company in Europe. Unipart now employs five times more people than when he started as CEO and turns over one billion pounds per year.

As in business, the non-conformist route can reap rewards in science as well. **Professor Malcolm Young** is one of just eighteen scientists worldwide to be nominated by *The Sunday Times* as the 'Brains behind the 21st Century'. Professor Young is the founder of e-Therapeutics, a firm that applies new concepts for treating human diseases.

Professor Young is a pioneer in the relatively new field of Network Pharmacology, which argues that to treat diseases we must understand the whole network of proteins and cells in the body, rather than target just a single protein. This approach is analogous to targeting a motorway junction to fix a problem rather than just one road.

e-Therapeutics has developed unique computers and algorithms to analyse protein networks. The team then test drug molecules that have the best overall impact on the network of proteins (or motorway junction) for a particular disease. The company is successfully discovering more effective drug treatments with staggering success rates.

Interestingly, Professor Young has achieved remarkable success in an important area by boldly going against decades of perceived wisdom in the pharmaceutical industry. In many respects, he has been dismantling the fundamental beliefs that have driven these huge firms for decades. For his ideas to succeed required more than just scientific brilliance – it required pursuing an unconventional path.

"In 2001," Professor Young explains, "I started looking in detail at what everybody else was doing in the pharma discovery industry. They were focused on this 'Magic Bullet' idea, which I thought you could show, definitively, was mistaken. I thought I was right and I thought that everybody else was wrong."

Professor Young's certainty in his argument against the perceived wisdom of the day is vivid. "I don't see it as a leap of faith. I see leaps of faith as leaps in the dark, where faith is required because there is no rational basis for where you have gone. My experiments were clear. Whenever you affect biology, you are affecting more than one thing. That didn't require any leap of faith. It required paying attention to what the data said, even though what the data said was inimical to the existing paradigm. Honestly, I had the annoying belief that I was right and I never doubted that."

Professor Young's biggest hurdle was securing funding – getting people to invest in his revolutionary new approach was a challenge. "The darkest moments were at the very start when it looked like no-one would have any interest," he says. "Our approach was absolutely left-field. I would talk to people in the traditional world of drug discovery and they didn't understand what we were doing. What has happened subsequently is that the tide has risen. It is no longer left-field. Now, it is pretty hard to find people who don't know what we are doing."

This kind of tidal shift hasn't been easy to achieve. "The physicist Thomas Kuhn's idea was that you only get a paradigm shift when proponents of the old one die," Young explains. "I think that is probably right." The difficulties of changing mind-sets was compounded by the vested interests that accompanied the old model. "Big pharma companies' R&D is a very risky environment," explains Professor Young. "It has shrunk mark-edly over the last five years and we represent an existential threat." The result has been a shift in approach for e-Therapeutics. "In general, I have adapted to the difficulty of interfacing with big pharma discovery by becoming self-sufficient," he admits. "We have enough resources to do everything that we need to do in the discovery and early development stage. By the time that you have knocked the spots off of a discovery candidate in early development, where it has a good activity profile, a good safety profile and is deliverable, it does not really matter to them – big pharma companies – where it has come from. I think we have adapted to that difficulty by becoming a self-sufficient drug discovery and development outfit."

There is an against-the-odds conviction to Professor Young that echoed that of John Neill as both have gone against the grain with radical ideas and produced spectacular results accordingly. But what was crucial to Professor Young's success? "Trusting my own scientific judgement is the one thing," he says. "My gratitude for the opportunity to have done that is to the Royal Society. They funded my research but there were almost no specifications of what I should do. It suited me and

I got used to being able to follow my own scientific nose. The confidence in the face of everyone disagreeing with me was really a function of that. Trust your data and trust your own intuition."

*   *   *

For the *Great Britons* who embrace risks, live in the discomfort zone or challenge the status quo, self-belief seems to compound within them. A virtuous circle ensues where successful risk-takers are infused with self-belief, leading to further risk-taking which in turn generates greater self-belief. In other words, *boldness* leading to emboldening.

Lauren Cuthbertson, who demonstrated her capacity for *grit* earlier, is an example of *boldness* fuelling self-belief. In training sessions under the watchful eye of her coach she persistently embraced the discomfort zone and pushed her body to new limits. "What I loved was that he pushed me to my limits but I didn't really find any," she says. "At a young age it filled me with confidence and belief, especially given I wasn't the most talented in the class. It made me realise that I could do so much more."

Lauren suggests this mindset was crucial to her success: "I had this inner belief my whole life. I never doubted for a second that I wouldn't do what I wanted to do. I was never big headed or boastful. I was middle of the class but I just knew that somehow it would happen."

For Lauren the idea of limits are now meaningless. Compared to most sports, dance is more nuanced. "It's much easier, when you're younger, to determine what's better," she says. "As you get older, it's much harder, because most professional people have a good base layer of technique. What you do with that makes you become the artist you become or the artist you don't become. And that's where it becomes an art form. People book to see different dancers because it's like going to see a gallery to see different artists you like. You can see the same ballet, even with the same steps, but it can look completely different with a different dancer."

Like Lauren, **Major Phil Ashby** is happy to be pushed. Ashby's career encapsulates many of the various elements of the *boldness* trait: taking risks, living in the discomfort zone, pushing himself and a profound confidence. "I thought long and hard about doing things that are physically difficult or potentially quite dangerous," he says. "In the military, it's part of the job description. But now, as a mountain guide, when I take people climbing some of them are, frankly, as scared as they've ever been. But I say to people to look deeper and realise they are doing this precisely *because* of the risk involved. In 21st Century Europe, life is fundamentally safe and can be a bit boring. I firmly believe that only by experiencing a bit of hardship and a bit of danger can you feel one hundred per cent alive. It's only by getting out of your comfort zone that you actually live and succeed.

"If you're in a position where you have to lead people and you're nervous, as long as you're giving the impression of being cool, calm and collected, that will rub off on other people. Because you're cool, calm and collected, they'll start being the same and everybody performs better.

"The ability to realise that prolonged physical hardship and discomfort doesn't kill you is important. It gives you a mental resolve and a toughness that, in a military setting, is vital, but is also applicable in other walks of life. You know that when setbacks happen you can cope and that gives you a lot of confidence."

You couldn't get two more different walks of life than a ballerina and a marine, yet their approach to life is strikingly similar. Both know the benefits and belief to be gained from being bold.

Chapter 3

Case Study: Simon Woodroffe

"I've always been creative and looked for new ideas but I knew conveyor belt sushi was a really good one. It was well established in Japan but all the chefs over here had been too scared to do it."

Simon Woodroffe, the hugely successful businessman and creator of YO! Sushi, is someone who knows all about *boldness*. Without it the restaurant chain he founded would never have developed into the household brand that it has become today. His restaurants created a totally new dining experience with novelties such as call buttons, robotic drinks trolleys and self-heating plates. Simon's success is built on traits such as *passion* and *grit*, yet it is the trait of *boldness* that truly encapsulates him.

When Simon came up with the idea of YO! Sushi he was intent on being bold from the outset. "I knew being outrageous was important to attract attention. The quality had to be high but we still had to attract attention. To do this we installed conveyor belts, automatic talking systems to order food and robots to deliver drinks. As a result, people wanted to go and see it and talk about it. It was novelty on a large scale. One way of starting would have been to do a small one to see if it worked but, then again, you've got to do something big enough that it creates the sense of an event."

Even so, opening a restaurant was extremely high risk. "The most difficult thing, and the thing I'm also most proud of, was to open the first restaurant," Simon says. "That took two years to do. I put in everything I had. It was an extremely insecure period but we opened the restaurant and it was successful within ten days."

Financing was a key problem as Simon personally lacked the money to get the project off the ground while his lack of experience in the restaurant business made investors naturally wary of lending to him. "I didn't have any money," he admits. "I had £200,000 tied up in my flat and I realised that I would have to put all of that on the line. Without that on the line, nobody else would be willing to invest money. I had no track record in the restaurant business."

Much like George Bullard described not being afraid of failing, Simon also learnt that failure was part and parcel of taking risks. "It really is true that you have to fail numerous times," he says, "and every time you fail or get rejected you accept that it's not personal and you just move on."

Simon's self-belief became crucial in seeing the project through. "I went through that year trying to put YO! Sushi together and watching my money running down and wondering if I was making a mistake," he says. "When you are committed to something, there is an incredible power to it. In spite of moments of terror, for the most part, there's a belief. And when you believe in something other people start to believe you."

This echoes Phil Ashby's comments that self-belief rubs off on other people and generates a virtuous circle of belief. Simon describes it as a magical formula. "If you're going to sell something," he stresses, "go out and find something which you believe in."

Simon believes one of the reasons behind the *boldness* of his ideas is because he left school so young and didn't have the imagination educated out of him. "I left school with GCSEs – or O levels as they were called in my day – so I wasn't very well educated and was ignorant about some of the things that lay ahead," he admits. "If I'd trained as an accountant or a lawyer I probably wouldn't have done anything as bold. I haven't been indoctrinated by society, as it were, as much as other people. It makes me imaginative. I certainly don't feel the need to do things just because they've been done in a normal way. I aspire to not being normal rather than conforming."

Again, the interplay between *boldness* and self-belief is apparent: Simon has the confidence to think differently, which, in turn, generates self-belief. This attitude of doing things differently is backed up with a fearless mindset and a belief that everything's possible. "When I say 'fearless'," he explains, "that doesn't mean 'without fear'. It's about feeling the fear and doing it anyway." Interestingly, Simon doesn't see himself as a risk taker. "Everybody has always labelled me as a risk taker and it took me a long time to realise that I had even taken any risks, because to me it felt like I didn't have an option. I put myself in situations where things had to be done and I suppose those were, technically, risks."

Similar to ocean rower Roz Savage, Simon deliberately forces himself into challenging situations. Furthermore, much like dancer Lauren Cuthbertson describes, he feels he has no limits. "I've been ambitious," Simon says. "The difference between my old business and YO! Sushi is that I aimed higher. As you get the confidence you aim higher and higher."

Simon's belief in being bold, taking risks and embracing fear is inspiring. "When you're out there swimming in shark infested waters and you feel comfortable there is definitely a sense of achievement," he says. "Even though you step outside your comfort zone and enter uncharted waters, there's an inner confidence. As Rudyard Kipling said, 'If you can keep your head when all around are losing theirs ...'."

Trait 5

A CONSTRUCTIVE CONSCIOUSNESS

Chapter 1

Case Study: Karen Darke

"I think a lot of fear is invented by our own minds. Fear is just our perception of something. If you can change your perception, then the fear is diminished. Fear stops us and holds us back. I don't ignore it, I try and use it in a helpful way."

When Karen Darke was just twenty-one she had an accident that changed her life forever. Whilst rock climbing, she fell and was left paralysed from the chest downwards. Remarkably, this didn't deter Karen from embarking on an array of extraordinary expeditions. She has crossed mountains in Central Asia on a hand bike, completed a 600 kilometre journey across Greenland on a sit-ski, climbed the one kilometre high rock face of El Capitan, in Yosemite National Park and won Paralympic gold in Rio in 2016.

It's a staggering list of achievements accomplished via great physical determination, mental strength and courage. "I have always been like that, but I don't know where it comes from. When I was a kid, I used to spend hours and hours doing my homework. At the end of the first year of school, I realised I couldn't keep working like that but I was worried that if I stopped working so hard then my marks would go down. I seem to set myself really high standards and goals. I like the challenge of it and, most of the time, I enjoy it. But sometimes I overcook it and that's why I fell off that cliff. If I didn't push myself I wouldn't have been up there that day trying to do what I was doing."

Despite that accident, Karen's outlook hasn't diminished at all. "I never learn," she laughs, "I keep doing it."

For Karen, it is as though no obstacle, large or small, is insurmountable. "For example, this morning I got up at five and flew to London City airport," she says. "It felt like there was just one obstacle after another to get from the airport and across London to this gym, which I had specifically found for training. Then the lifts weren't working and it was a nightmare. It's non-stop obstacles every day when you're in a wheelchair. If I let obstacles stop me I wouldn't really do very much.

"In fact, the thing that stops a lot of people with disabilities going on outdoor adventures is toilet facilities, which is a massive issue. I suppose I've always thought of innovative ways to make it work. I've probably made compromises that some people might not be prepared to make. Without getting too personal, I would just shove a catheter in so that it doesn't really matter where I am. I can go anywhere then."

Karen's attitude shines through. "Clearly it means there are things that I can't do easily," she says, recalling her accident. "But I've always had the philosophy that, if you sit around feeling miserable about it, or feel frustrated by it, or focus on what you can't do, then you're not going to live a very happy life. I tend to focus on what I *can* do.

"It wasn't an easy process in the beginning. I did spend time thinking about what I couldn't do with friends which I could do before. As a result, your friends change a little bit because you, naturally, get involved in other things. My attitude is to make the most of it."

Karen sees her attitude as an instinctive one and an approach borne out of positive sentiments. "It's not driven by any sort of anger," she says. "It's purely driven by a love of experiences. I love learning. I love having experiences. I think you could probably call me an experience junkie. Some people think I'm some kind of expedition junkie but I think it's not really about that. It's more that I love learning about different things, different places, people and environments."

Yet, for all this positive thinking, Karen's confidence and self-belief remains fragile. She admits to regularly being full of fear and self-doubt. "How do I overcome it? Something inside me still drives me to do it even though I feel scared. I try and use the fear to help me do it more safely. I often end up writing a list of all my fears and concerns and then think about what I could do to feel better about each of them. The fear becomes part of the planning process. Fear, to me, stands for 'False Expectations Appearing Real'. I often deconstruct fear and reconstruct it in a better way. Like climbing El Capitan, I had to deconstruct what was going on in my head the whole time to get in a place where I could not be so fearful and do it. There was a massive fear of heights, which I never had when I used to climb."

Karen describes that climb as a powerful experience in facing a fear and overcoming it. "I had the opportunity to leave and go on a Californian beach holiday instead," she remembers. "But I didn't want to. It's a classic example of my character. I wanted to go back to El Capitan and figure it out. There was some stuff to figure out practically, like how to use a team of people to climb when one of them is paralysed, but the bigger part of it was figuring it out mentally and how to change my perception of what I was doing.

"I think when you feel fear it's like watching a horror movie playing in your head. I would never choose to watch a horror movie, so it is a choice to turn it off and start playing a new movie. I think it is as simple as that."

In fact, Karen became so curious about the mind that she ended up delving even deeper. "I've studied hypnotherapy," she reveals, "and when you look at a person thinking in a certain way you can see that the brain lights up in a specific way and when they change their thoughts it lights up in a different way. Just like you get used to moving your body in a certain way you get used to moving your mind in a certain way and certain neural pathways firing in the brain. Often they can be unhelpful, like fear, but you can stop them by making a choice. I think anything that shifts your perspective, and it can be subtle, can make a big difference."

For Karen, this strength of mind and being able to shift perspective has been crucial in her various endurance challenges: "I think in all the big endurance stuff I've done, like skiing across Greenland, which physically was probably one of the hardest things I've ever done, if I had focused on the pain in my body, or focused on how tired I was, or how hard it all was, then it just becomes torture.

"I've got a little saying which is, 'the freedom of curiosity', I find that if I'm experiencing a difficult situation I focus on thinking about the fact that I had never been this high before, or this tired before, or I wonder what's going to happen next. By doing this it shifts your perspective. If you can stay curious and be in the moment as much as possible, rather than focusing on how far it is, how long it is, how hard it is, then I think it helps."

Being in the moment is part of Karen's mindset in undertaking these challenges. "My enjoyment and motivation isn't about achievement," she says. "It's about the experience of being there in that moment. I don't really have an achievement checklist in my head."

This state of mind and being in the moment is what Karen craves. "Generally, I find it hard to be lost in day to day life," she continues, "because you've got a schedule, appointments, clocks or things you've got to do. Whereas, when I embark on a big challenge or expedition, time seems to become irrelevant.

"You can become completely lost in it because all that matters is keeping going and, at some point, getting some sleep, warmth and food. It simplifies life. It removes all distraction. Probably my next level of mastery will be doing that with everyday life!"

For all her achievements, it is coping with her situation that stands out for Karen as the most difficult thing she's done. "I often say the hardest physical thing I've ever done is skiing across Greenland and the hardest mental thing is climbing El Capitan," she says, "but that's probably not true. The hardest physical and mental thing I've ever done is getting through the process of being paralysed.

"It's not something I've ever felt proud of but, reflecting on it recently, I realised that it's something I took for granted. I don't think I should have because there's lots of people who end up with serious disabilities who don't manage to build a fun, positive life. They become part of the medical system and don't get through that. I like it that I don't take any medication and never visit doctors. People assume that, because you're in a wheelchair, you're going to need loads of medication and it's not true. I'm proud of that."

Chapter 2

Interpreting Events and Choosing your Mindset

While each of the Britons interviewed exhibit a few specific traits that define them, they have all shown elements of one final attribute, a trait that, in many ways, encompasses all the others.

They all exhibit a *constructive consciousness*, which means, firstly, that the individuals are constructive in their interpretations of life's events and, secondly, this way of thinking is a conscious decision on behalf of the individual. In other words, to approach the world in this manner is a choice.

Karen Darke is an excellent example of someone who embodies a *constructive consciousness* with her attitude of making the most out of any given situation. Furthermore, she talks about fear being a mental construct that can be deconstructed and reconstructed, akin to a film playing in the brain that needs ejecting and replacing with another one.

Looking back over the various interviewees it is clear that mindset is critical. What is fundamental to so many of these success stories is adopting a constructive interpretation of life's events and these case studies show anyone can choose to think in this way.

There are many elements in life that are beyond one's control such as one's genes, family members or economic climate. Nonetheless, one thing that can be controlled is how to interpret the events we face on any given day. As Guy Disney says, "Bad things happen to everyone, without a doubt. Everybody will have a sad story in their life. It is completely naïve to think you are the only person with something bad going on in your world. It is how you get on with it that is the real test."

Time and again, the *Great Britons* in this book have learned to control their internal experience (like Karen Darke and fear) so they can maximise their external experiences (climbing El Capitan despite being paralysed). This constructive interpretation of events seems ingrained for some *Great Britons* and, for others, it is triggered by adverse events or trauma – but for all of them it is present in some shape or form.

Constructive Interpretation of Events

To begin with, it's important to look at the constructive element of a *constructive consciousness* by focusing on particular examples of this effective thinking. Three specific examples of constructive thinking stand out; mindfulness, turning adversity into opportunity and the interpretation of luck.

In conversation, Guy Disney stresses that he believes that he made his own luck and that, the more he practised, the luckier he got. This was a sentiment echoed by Michael Acton-Smith and other interviewees like Linzi Boyd who believes: "Opportunities are presented on your life journey and then out of those you create your own luck." Each time, a positive interpretation of luck emerged from the *Great Britons*.

Whether creating their own luck or perceiving themselves as lucky, the message from the *Great Britons* is always a constructive interpretation of luck. Either luck is on their side or it is a factor they deliberately tilted in their favour via practise and the pursuit of opportunity. Perhaps the person who discusses luck the most is jockey AP McCoy. "I've been lucky in so many ways," he said. McCoy describes becoming Champion Jockey in his first season, the numerous wins he has had and even the calibre of people he has worked with as being down to luck. "I've always been lucky to be able to convince myself that me winning is going to happen."

Ironically, his achievements, overall, have little to do with luck. One of the reasons AP McCoy is particularly proud of his record as Champion Jockey is because the title recognises excellence and consistency. While there might be an element of luck in any individual race, over the course of a season any fortune is likely to even out. When McCoy goes through his 'lucky' incidents, it is quickly apparent that many of them are, in fact, not to do with fortune. For example, winning the Totesport Trophy immediately after falling off his horse in the previous race was down to his determination to get back in the saddle and carry on. What's more, his positivity is central to his success, no more so than his ability to ignore any negative media coverage he has had.

McCoy has made his own luck. By putting himself in the position of being able to compete and have the option of winning time and again, McCoy is always improving his chances.

There is a distinction to be drawn between being fortunate and being lucky. Chrissie Wellington is someone who captures this difference particularly well. "I think I was fortunate to have been born into a family where there were opportunities, with parents that wanted me to get an education and who were willing to support me through that," she says. "I do, however, think that I made conscious choices for myself that meant I've been able to succeed. I don't think that's luck. I think I've carved out my own path. 'Lucky' implies that fate has handed you success. I don't believe in that. I think I made a conscious decision to go to university. I made a conscious decision to study International Development. I made that difficult decision to become a professional athlete. I don't think that that was based on luck and I don't think it was predetermined."

Indeed, a number of the *Great Britons* have been fortunate but that would undervalue their dedication, determination and their commitment to putting themselves in a position where opportunities arise.

"You know," Simon Woodroffe says, "I definitely think you get moments of luck but the more you do, and the more consistent you are, the more things just fall into place more easily.

"I'm a great believer in the sowing of seeds, so to speak. In years to come you might have something I could do to help you, or vice versa. So those seeds are very important and you've got to go out and sow them and, out of those seeds, luck can grow. You can definitely make your own luck."

Tutor Mark Maclaine is someone whose experiences sum up the second example of constructive thought: turning adversity, failure and mistakes into a positive. "I feel fortunate to have had bad things happen to me in my life because they led me to want to get out and want to change," he says. At first glance, his belief feels almost counter-intuitive. Most people would think that being fortunate would involve good things happening to you, rather than the opposite. But for Mark, adverse events are the best way for him to learn and improve.

"I'm very open when I make mistakes," he explains, "that's been the greatest lesson I've learnt. When I make mistakes I don't chastise myself. That's probably been my greatest belief system that's allowed me to learn and grow and do the job I'm doing even when I get something wrong when tutoring."

Yet, Mark hasn't always followed this approach. "I wasn't always like that," he admits. "When I was younger, I saw mistakes as terrible and was desperate to cover them all up. I didn't want to live in reality. I lived in a make-believe world until my mid-teens just to protect myself from the environment that I was actually in, like not having a father or the bullying at school. The only way I coped was creating a make-believe world and there was no way I could ever become successful in that.

"It was actually when I ripped two ligaments in my left knee and ended up spending three months in bed that I really thought about life and started to realise that, actually, I was doing it all wrong. Everything changed after that and I started embracing failure as a potential for success. When I fail is when I learn. Now I encourage my students not to see it as failure, per se, but see it as something in life that happens and something that helps us grow."

It is striking to see the positive demeanour the *Great Britons* have in the face of adversity, failure and mistakes. From Ironman champion Chrissie Wellington to businesswoman Linzi Boyd, they all see mistakes as opportunities to learn.

Simon Woodroffe takes it even further to get results. "I would force myself to pitch my idea to six people in the space of a week," he says. "If I'd had five failures and time was running out at the end of the week, I would go up to people in the street and politely ask to pitch my idea. I've done that and people have actually helped me out. In fact, in Japan they don't even have a word for 'good luck' – their equivalent saying is 'keep going'."

There's an old adage amongst entrepreneurs that failure is the million dollar MBA. While failure is a well-known lesson in business, the *Great Britons* show that equanimity can be applied to any sphere of life. "I prefer to call it a learning experience rather than a mistake," says Roz Savage when asked about the subject. "I do my best not to make the same mistake twice and to always learn something from the experience. As a child I was always afraid of making a mistake. I was cursed by having done well at school and so I became terrified of failure, which pretty much guarantees a life of mediocrity. If you want to get stuff done and live boldly you have to be willing to make mistakes from time to time – it's how you know you're pushing the envelope."

It's an important point that is echoed by Chrissie Wellington: "Setbacks happen and the route to success is never like going up a ladder. It's like a climbing frame where you're trying to get around problems. Whilst we don't always want adversity, in the end, it makes us stronger. It enables us to retain perspective and learn. It means we take a step back and think about how we might do things better. We get complacent and that's never a good thing. Adversity, although it's painful, doesn't usually last forever and if you don't experience it you won't open your eyes to new things."

The third example of constructive thought displayed across the *Great Britons* is a sense of mindfulness or, in other words, a sense of living in the moment, being present and appreciative. Karen Darke, the Paralympian, exemplifies this mindset. Jamie McDonald learnt the advantages of living in the moment from his injury-ridden run across Canada. Pen Hadow puts it philosophically when describing his isolation on his journey to the North Pole: "It's like a secular pilgrimage. In living like a monk, one may be able to reach a higher level of understanding." Indeed, the mindfulness displayed by many of the *Great Britons* encompasses a level-headedness and understanding of gratitude that wouldn't be out of place in a religious sentiment.

Jockey AP McCoy, in particular, knows the importance of keeping a level head. "You should never let praise or criticism get to you," he says. "It is a weakness to get caught up in either. I've had a lot of good things written about me but, like everyone, you get negative things written about you as well. I've always been able to keep it level no matter what."

Taken together, this mindfulness offers a straightforward approach to life: appreciative of what you have, appreciative of the help of others and appreciative of the moment. "You only get to live once," reiterates Major Phil Ashby, recalling his harrowing time in hospital with an inflamed spinal cord, "and, personally, I think life is better if you're seeing the positives."

Choosing your Mindset

"I think some people are negative," Guy Disney says. "While some are positive and others are practical. If you feel happy or sad, you can always try and influence that. I think mindset is a choice, it's about discipline. It's a stubbornness and I think everybody can be stubborn if they want to be."

The second component of a *constructive consciousness*, which is a common thread through all the *Great Britons*, is the element of choice – the conscious decision to adopt such an approach. "It's definitely your choice," AP McCoy stresses. "Once I had been Champion Jockey five or six times, I had the choice to relax. But I chose not to."

"I think adopting a mindset is a choice," Chrissie Wellington adds. "For example, retirement has been an incredibly challenging process psychologically. When I retired there were days where I would wallow in self-pity, questioning my identity and value. I would consciously kick myself up the arse and realise I had a choice. You have a choice to be happy and to see how blessed and privileged you've been, or you can be sombre and make your life and everyone else's life a misery. You consciously pull yourself into line and make that choice to be positive and optimistic."

Roz Savage goes further. "We do have a choice in the way we respond to situations. You choose whether you're going to be a victim or whether you're going to transcend it. I love Viktor Frankl's book *Man's Search for Meaning* and you can't imagine a worse situation than being in a concentration camp for years. Yet, he was so dignified in the way that he chose to respond to that situation – he looked at what he could contribute to his fellow prisoners and how he could make their lives better. He didn't get wrapped up in his own drama of family members he'd lost or how much he was hungry or in pain. What an amazing role model Viktor Frankl is.

"Being in a concentration camp makes rowing an ocean look like a complete walk in the park. At least I had the chance to choose my trials. In parallel with that, when I was rowing the Atlantic, I often thought about Harbo and Samuelsen, the two guys who, in 1896, rowed across the North Atlantic, which is much worse than where I crossed in the Mid-Atlantic. It's colder and has more capricious currents and wind and they didn't have any of the technical gear I had, like a watertight cabin. I never complained when I thought of them."

Many of the *Great Britons* give specific examples of when a changed mindset has helped change their course for the better. Lauren Cuthbertson altered her attitude early on in her ballet career. "I realised that my career was plateauing," she admits, "and I just wasn't being given the roles." After a period of frustration, Lauren made the choice to change her perspective and adopt a totally new attitude. "I didn't know why they weren't giving me the roles," she says. "But I suddenly switched how I approached it and was more disciplined and decided to stop pleading for roles. I decided to make myself the dancer that you *want* to give the roles to. I eliminated the fight and focused. Do it the best you can and make it so obvious that it is *your* role."

Pen Hadow, meanwhile, explains how he learnt to choose his mindset and deal with the challenges of a solo expedition. "I learnt from my solo Pole expeditions," he says, "when you're alone, the change in morale from 'everything is fine' to 'this is pointless and I'm giving up' can be rapid because the spiral down is not checked. There is nobody with you to reassure you or pull your sledge for an hour or navigate for an hour. There is no-one there to correct your downward spiral of thoughts. It's very fast, especially if you've got very low blood sugars, which you have a lot of the time. Ultimately, it's irrational."

Irrational as it might be, such thoughts can feel very real with goals seeming to recede into the distance. "On the way to the North Pole I would encounter pressure ridges and ice rubble fields that would go on for kilometre after kilometre," Pen continues. "It was crushed jagged ice as far as the eye could see, which can take days to negotiate. When you are trying to consistently cover at least 12 kilometres a day and you're hypoglycemic you become open to irrationality and rash decisions. I would curse my sledge, the expedition, why I was bothering. It quickly becomes very demoralising."

To counter this, Pen has come up with mental techniques to deal with this irrationality. "With the help of a psychologist, I worked out how to visualise myself in a music recording studio, with a wild rock band on the other side of the glass thrashing out heavy metal," he reveals. "But I am the recording engineer, in control with my feet up on the desk and behind the glass with headphones on happily listening to classical music ... so I had to remind myself, the heavy rock music was like the ice rubble that I had to negotiate. So, I can choose how I respond. It is a choice."

Pen's technique goes further: "Then, I go into an intellectual exercise and remind myself that no-one sent me here and this isn't a prison sentence. It's not a punishment. I have worked hard to raise the money and get everyone on board to get here. It's a privilege, not a punishment. The final step is to then recognise this isn't just a privilege. This is bloody it. This is *the* challenge. Anyone can pull a sledge for a few kilometres around the Pole but it's dealing with the other stuff that makes the challenge what it is. The environment has got nothing against you. It's terribly simple out there because I haven't got lots of people, teams, workmates or family. This is just you on a totally neutral plain – a blank sheet – and you can make it hell or heaven or whatever else. It's entirely in your head."

Out of all the traits, it is this final trait, a *constructive conscious-ness* that is both the most inspiring and the most far reaching in its scope. There is a universality to it in the way it encompasses all of the other traits, and a universality in its application – an approach to life that anyone can adopt, whether your challenges are epic or minor.

John Neill's musings about choices and mindset are particularly poignant. "You don't have thoughts, thoughts have you," he says, "I really like that phrase." As the *Great Britons* have all shown, the power of the human mind is remarkable if directed in a constructive manner and the possibilities of what can be achieved are seemingly limitless.

Chapter 3

Case Study: Karl Hinett

"It was 19 September 2005 and I was in the British Army as a part of the Staffordshire Regiment in Iraq. We had about three weeks left of our six-month tour and there was an incident where two British soldiers were captured and taken to a suspicious local police station. The information that we were getting was that they were going to be handed over to the local insurgents.

"We all presumed the worst and became part of the operation to free them. We worked alongside Special Forces and supported in our armoured Warrior vehicles. I was a gunner and operated the weapon systems of one of these vehicles. When we arrived on the scene it didn't look too bad although there must have been between 1,500 to 2,000 local people there. To begin with, a lot of them were just spectators and our job was to distract the crowd while the Special Forces went in to rescue the British soldiers.

"Then things changed. It started with a few kids throwing rocks at the Warriors and, as time wore on, they grew in confidence and in numbers and became more violent. Small rocks turned into bigger rocks and it escalated almost instantly. Large rocks then became petrol bombs. Before I knew it, I was completely doused in petrol and a second later I was alight.

"I remember the fire completely engulfing the inside of the turret and, because of the minimal space in it, the heat and flames became intense. I kept calm for what must have been twenty seconds and then realised that, if I wanted to survive, I had to summon up all my strength and energy to pull myself out while on fire."

Karl Hinett's life was to change irrevocably after his harrowing ordeal in Basra, Iraq. It is difficult to underline how close to death he was as the petrol bomb attack turned him into a human fireball. That he managed to pull himself out of the Warrior armoured vehicle is testament to a number of things, not least his presence of mind and control of his thoughts to drag himself out. But getting out of the vehicle was just the first step on a hugely difficult journey for him.

"My hands took a lot of damage when I gripped onto the burning metal of the Warrior to pull myself out," he recalls. "As I managed to lift myself clear, I momentarily blacked out. I woke up when I hit the floor and luckily my friends were there with fire extinguishers. They carried me back to an ambulance, which was waiting much further away in a safe area.

"I still remember everything clearly. I was administered morphine and I looked down at my body and all my clothes were in tatters. I still had my boots on. From mid-thigh down to my boot was all rags and tattered clothing and burns. I had my Kevlar body armour on but from my fingertips to my shoulders was all damaged clothing and burns. I felt it on my face as well but, as soon as I was put down into the back of the ambulance, the medics started pouring water over me to cool my body down. It wasn't freezing-cold water because that would have spattered uncontrollably.

"I must have been in the ambulance for about twenty minutes, being kept awake by the medics until the helicopter came to pick me up and take me back to a field hospital. I remember everything right up until getting taken into the hospital, having a needle injected into my foot and having a mask put over my face and put to sleep."

Karl was put into an induced coma for ten days. He underwent two twelve-hour operations and one nine-hour one as the surgeons dealt with effects of the heat and burns – he had suffered severe burns that required skin grafting. When Karl came to he was unable to move and walk around because of various machines hooked up to his body. He remained stationary for ten days and around forty per cent of his burnt body was an open wound. The stress and the effect of his body trying to recover meant he wasted muscle mass rapidly.

"When I did come to," he remembers, "I'd lost so much weight. I think I got down to just over eight stone."

Nonetheless, Karl's rationale and reaction to his injuries were remarkable. "When I woke up, I sort of knew," he says. "Straightaway, I accepted what had happened because I remembered so much of it. Because there was no question about what had happened, it actually made it easier to recovery mentally.

"From the moment that I woke up I knew what the surgeons had done was irreversible and I knew, regardless of how well or how badly recovery goes, that burns leave behind an horrific injury. So, in my mind, there was no way to go other than forward because if I dwelt on the injury that I had I would never get anywhere in life."

Both in the petrol bomb attack itself and in coming to terms with what happened, Karl's *constructive consciousness* and his ability to take control of events is inspiring. It is easy to forget that recovery from any serious injury is more than just a physical process. "There were a few things that I knew I had to get a grip with in those early days post-injury," Karl says. "I knew that I'd just returned from a job with responsibility in a highly hostile environment to, all of a sudden, being bedbound with no independence at all and needing help for even the simplest of tasks. I've read enough stories about post-traumatic stress and succumbing to the dark side of injury that, if I didn't have something to occupy myself or something to really focus on, then I could easily fall into depression.

"That's not saying that I didn't have bad days, because there definitely were some, but it was understanding that it was a work in progress; like starting back at the beginning again. The first step was to get onto my feet and walking."

The rehabilitation process to be able to walk again, and then run, became central to his physical and mental recovery. "As my recovery went on and the more strength I regained, I took to running on a treadmill," he remembers. "It was difficult at first but the simple act of moving forward physically was almost reinforcing what I had in my mind of moving forward in recovery. That's what eventually turned into long-distance running over the years. It really helps as a form of therapy. Research shows it's an antidepressant, a stress reliever and good for your body – so running became my focus. Whenever I felt like I was having a bad day, or even remotely starting to feel sorry for myself, I'd go for a run and it put me back onto the right track."

Running for recovery, however, was just the beginning for Karl. In spring 2007, less than two years after the attack in Basra, Karl completed the London Marathon. Since then, he has set himself the challenge of completing a remarkable 200 marathons by the time he is thirty. So far, Karl has completed over 100 marathons and he is well on target to achieve his goal. In the process, he has raised tens of thousands of pounds for the burns unit at the Queen Elizabeth Hospital in Birmingham (the successor to the Selly Oak Hospital, where he was treated). He has run marathons on five continents, including the North Pole and Antarctica races. He also trained for a climb of Mount Everest with other wounded soldiers, although the expedition was eventually called off due to avalanches.

Completing such challenges is as much down to the mind as the body. For Karl, it felt as though he was running without limits. "After completing fifty-two marathons in a year, I didn't think I'd ever reach a limit," he says. "It's what you believe in yourself, isn't it? I've never felt that I've reached a limit because reaching a limit in anything physical or sporting would have to mean me passing out. I always say to myself at the start of running a marathon that if I can't run it, I'll walk, and if I can't walk it, I'll crawl. You can always take your time. It's amazing how much your body can endure. Compared to your mind, your body is not going to give up that easy."

Conclusion

This study into the behaviour and beliefs that fuel *Great Britons* to remarkable feats was set in motion by a single interview with a wounded soldier. Captain Guy Disney overcame great personal challenges from the attack he suffered in Afghanistan and has gone on to achieve remarkable feats, including expeditions to the North and South Pole. It seems fitting to conclude with the story of another wounded soldier, Karl Hinett.

In between these two soldiers, an array of *Great Britons*, from a ballerina to a sushi magnate and from Paralympians to entrepreneurs, all have diverse stories to tell. From Olympic medallists to CEOs, I have come away from my meetings in awe of the various people I have met. It is refreshing and inspiring to interact with so many people embracing life so vociferously and to see, at first hand, the almost boundless possibilities of human endeavour.

"I have been lucky to meet people who have that mindset," Guy told me when we first spoke. I now recognise those are words I can utter myself upon completing this book. It has been a privilege to share their incredible stories.

From meeting all these truly great Britons I have discovered their attitudes to life are remarkably similar. The striking similarities between their personality traits shone through during the interviews. While I am in awe of every Briton in this book, I am also encouraged to discover that these five traits can be used as a framework for anyone to guide themselves towards their own personal Mount Everest. The insights from this study should leave us all buoyed with the belief that remarkable feats are accessible as long as the right mindset is in place and that these traits are not bestowed on the lucky few by divine intervention.

In light of the different attitudes we have uncovered it seems fitting to give the last word to Guy Disney, the man who inspired this project.

"I think mindset is a choice and it's about discipline. That's the way I think. I react badly when events go well and I react well when they go badly. It sounds counterintuitive but when things are going badly it tends to bring out the best in people. In Afghanistan I came across some of the most unpleasant people that exist. Yet, I also saw some of the very best human beings confronting them. I saw children who had had their hands cut off and being made to do things by the Taliban that were inherently evil, while I also saw the best of our society, in the British Army, engaging with that.

"You need to have the right mindset and then take advantage of it. I have very little sympathy for people who are not moving forward. Bad things happen to everyone, without a doubt. It is completely naïve to think that you are the only person with something bad going on in your world. But it is how you get on with it that is the real test of a person's character."

It is no easy task to distil Guy's myriad of inspiring words down. Indeed, that is true for all the individuals whom I have been fortunate to spend time with. Ultimately, intrinsic motivation and *passion* are the nucleus of any remarkable achievement. Once a *passion* is ignited, an intense level of *grit*, determination and fortitude are needed to carry it through. Along the path to achieving any remarkable feat there is, inevitably, fierce *competitiveness* with others as well as yourself. One's resolve is tested relentlessly but impediments can be overcome by *boldness* in ideas or actions.

Overall, it is the power of human cognition that is the crucial insight from this study. The lessons from the *constructive*

140

consciousness chapter are powerful. We can all constructively interpret our life events in order to be more mindful, to live in the moment, to consider ourselves lucky or grateful, to grow from our mistakes and not be afraid of failure. In the end, we can all choose the mindset we adopt.

Some of these stories may inspire readers more than others but these constructive insights are lessons we can all benefit from. The *Great Britons* in this book have used such a mindset to overcome great personal challenges but we can all adapt our thinking to pursue our own dreams, whatever they might be. While I have drawn on the quotes and insights of the *Great Britons* I met in this book, it is a line from another truly great Briton that perfectly encapsulates the spirit of what I have learnt:

> *"There is nothing either good nor bad, but thinking makes it so."*
>
> William Shakespeare

If you have learnt one lesson from this book,
buy one more copy for a friend.
By doing so you will support one more wounded soldier.

List of Great Britons:

Anthony (AP) McCoy: twenty-time Champion Jockey. Grand National winner and Sports Personality of the Year 2010.

Chrissie Wellington: four-time Ironman World Champion and world record holder.

Eliza Rebeiro: founder of the charity Lives Not Knives. Founded the charity aged thirteen.

George Bullard: extreme adventurer and world record holder. World record for the longest unsupported journey across Antarctica without resupply (113 days and 1,374miles).

Gilo Cardozo: engineer who designed a paramotor that Bear Grylls flew over Everest. Also designed a flying car which he flew/drove from London to Timbuktu.

Heather Fell: World Champion and Olympic silver medallist in the sport of Modern Pentathlon.

James Rhodes: professional concert pianist with six albums released so far and presenter of various programmes on Channel 4, BBC4 and Sky Arts.

Jamie McDonald: extreme adventurer and fundraiser. Cycled from Bangkok to his home town of Gloucester. Also holds the static cycling world record (268 hours 32 minutes and 44 seconds). In February 2014, became the first person in history to run unsupported across Canada.

John Neill: the CEO and Chairman of Unipart Group. John has led the company for over thirty years making him the longest serving CEO of any major company in Europe.

Karen Darke: 2016 Paralympic gold medallist, Paratriathalon World Champion and ground breaking adventurer.

Karl Hinett: wounded soldier with forty per cent burns. Completed fifty-two marathons in fifty-two weeks. Now has completed over 150 marathons in total.

Kevin Godlington: former member of the Special Forces. The founder of a development company specialising in conflict and former conflict nations. Runs an orphanage in Sierra Leone.

Kirsty Henderson: British Champion and ranked number 1 in the world for Shidokan karate.

Lauren Cuthbertson: Principal dancer with the Royal Ballet. The position of Principal is the highest rank within the Royal Ballet and identifies Lauren as one of the leading dancers in the world.

Levison Wood: writer, photographer and explorer. Completed expeditions walking the length of the Nile and the length of the Himalayas.

Linzi Boyd: entrepreneur and founder of the Surgery Group. Author of *Brand Famous* and founder of Business of Brand School.

Malcolm Young: scientist and the founder of e-Therapeutics. The company is a pioneer in the field of network pharmacology, a distinctive approach to the discovery and development of medicines. He is one of just eighteen scientists worldwide nominated by *The Sunday Times* as the 'Brains behind the 21st Century'.

Mark Maclaine: one of the most experienced one to one tutors in the world. Completed over 18,000 hours of one to one tutoring in Maths and Science.

Michael Acton-Smith: the founder of the entertainment company Mind Candy and the creator of the global kids' phenomenon *Moshi Monsters*.

Patrick Veitch: professional gambler. Over a period of less than ten years he won over £10 million betting on horse racing.

Pen Hadow: first person ever to trek solo, without assistance or resupply, from Canada to the North Geographic Pole. A feat which has never been repeated since.

Phil Ashby: Royal Marine. Aged twenty-nine, was promoted to Major, the youngest person ever to hold that rank in the whole of the armed forces. Escaped capture in Sierra Leone and won the Queen's Medal for Gallantry.

Roz Savage: ocean rower and world record holder. Has rowed solo across the Atlantic, Pacific and Indian oceans. This equates to over 15,000 miles and around five million oar strokes.

Simon Woodroffe: the founder of YO! Sushi. Aside from creating YO! brands Simon mentors young entrepreneurs. He has appeared as a Dragon on the BBC programme *Dragon's Den*.

Tom James: double Olympic gold medallist, rowing. (2008, Beijing Olympics and 2012, London Olympics).

Acknowledgements

I am deeply grateful to all the *Great Britons* featured in this book. Without them I couldn't have uncovered the *Great Traits*. Every one of them generously sacrificed their time to be interviewed. Without exception, they were charming, charitable and captivating. This book would not have been possible without them. I am indebted to you all.

I'm honoured to help the charity *Walking With The Wounded* and sincerely thank Ed Parker for his support.

Publishing a book is a herculean task and the single moniker on the front cover belies the work of an army. My friend Nico Wills has brought the book to life with his skill behind the camera. I am endlessly grateful to him for committing so much time and effort to this project. I could not have formed the structure of the book without the skill and support of Tom Bromley. I am indebted to my editor, Edward Neale, who refined my sporadic thoughts. He is a man of letters and made this book far better than I could have done alone. Thanks to the team at Great Traits Publishing and the ingenious guidance of Rebecca Souster. Thanks to the creative wizard Mark Ecob for the cover design. Thanks to Helen Baggott for her meticulous proof reading.

A few people played a pivotal role in the making of this book. In particular, I am indebted to the brilliant clinical psychologist Charlotte Kerr for her introduction to qualitative research methods and Thematic analysis. Marc Burton was a crucial supporter of the book from its inception and his impact was immeasurable. Maura Brickell was beyond generous with her time and provided an endless stream of superb suggestions.

My sincere thanks go to her and Carly Cook for their support. Early drafts of the book were refined thanks to valuable feedback from Mattie Stockwell, George Viney, Peter Unwin, my brother Oliver and my parents. I am immensely grateful to you all.

While writing the book I was blessed to meet Louise Allen-Jones, Charlie Redmayne, John Bond, Autumn Green and Damian Barr. Thank you for sharing such sage advice.

Meeting the array of remarkable people featured in this book required the assistance of many friends. I would like to thank everyone listed here for their vital help in meeting the *Great Britons*: Eugenie Smith, James Emtage, Tom Barber, Harry Bullard, Dilly Nock, Ed Stockwell, Tom Arms, Ed and Henny Plunkett, George Ryan, Alex Neill, Tom Scudamore, David Redvers, Mikey Wilson, Storm and Rosie Green, Ellie Sharpe, Emma Collins, Camilla Harris, Tim Olivier and Simon Crane.

The only thing more taxing than writing a book is being married to someone who is writing a book. My most sincere and significant thanks go to my incredible wife Henrietta, my darling daughter Phoebe and our wondrous whippet Mole. I couldn't have done it without your support and I am forever grateful to have you all by my side.

APPENDIX

Methodology

Thematic analysis (Braun & Clarke, 2006) was used to derive the traits discussed in this book. Thematic analysis is a common form of qualitative research which examines and records patterns or themes within data. Thematic analysis uses six stages of coding to establish *if* patterns exist within the dataset. These phases are: familiarisation with data, generating initial codes, searching for themes among codes, reviewing themes, defining and naming themes, and producing the final report. Thematic analysis goes beyond simply counting phrases or words in a text and identifies implicit and explicit ideas within the data.

Each interview for *Great Traits* was conducted with predefined questions that were employed consistently. This tried to improve the accuracy of comparisons between the different sets of data. Questions were not always asked in the same order, to try and avoid fatigue bias. The interviewees were asked additional questions to elicit more content outside the pre-set questions meaning each interview followed a semi-structured format.

Questions were formed to try and reduce bias. While it is almost impossible to remove all bias, the composition of a question can have an impact on the likely answer. Questions which begin with "do you" "are you" "would you" all tend to lead to a narrow "yes" or "no" answer. Questions which begin with "what do you" "when do you" "how do you" offer a wider response. For example, the author deemed it less efficient to simply ask "are you determined?" or "do you have grit?" but preferable to ask "how do you react when things go badly?" or "tell me when you have overcome a setback".

Each interview was recorded and professionally transcribed. All interviews lasted between 45–90 minutes and led to transcripts of between 15–30 typed pages. The quotations in this book are taken from the transcripts of face-to-face interviews completed by the author. Additional sources such as books, articles, speeches and documentaries were used to inform the literature review for each individual interviewed but the data analysed were composed of the interview transcripts alone.

The *Great Traits* conclusions have attempted to be a grounded theory as they draw theoretical conclusions from the dataset. At the outset, no preconceived or predetermined frameworks were used.

Overall, thematic analysis offers a flexible research process which is well suited to large data sets. It allows for themes to be interpreted and supported by data. However, it does have disadvantages. There are limitations to this book which should be noted. In this instance:

- SUBJECTIVITY. Classifying a 'remarkable feat' is subjective. It can be quantified for some (e.g. Olympic medallist or World Champion) but for others it is a subjective judgment (e.g. devoting your time to help others/ form a charity).
- INTERVIEWEE SELECTION. We deliberately interviewed individuals from diverse genres (business, sport, the military, science, technology, charities and the arts) but the interviewees were in part driven by accessibility, speculative approaches and a degree of chance.
- OPPORTUNITY BIAS. The interviewees were deliberately chosen from diverse social and economic backgrounds but we do not assess the role of opportunity in our analysis.
- SURVIVORSHIP BIAS. There could easily be people who exhibit all of the *Traits* highlighted in this book without them attaining remarkable feats.
- INTERVIEW QUESTIONS. Questions were formed to reduce bias but no question can be completely without bias.
- INTERPRETATION. How individuals interpret themselves vs how others see them may be different.

Further work is required to address these topics and questions.

Further information on thematic analysis can be found in Braun, V. and Clarke, V. (2006) *Using thematic analysis in psychology*. Qualitative Research in Psychology, 3 (2). pp. 77–101.

About the Author

Tobias Harwood is the author of *Great Traits* and the founder of GreatTraitsProject.com. Since shattering his pelvis and fracturing his back aged seventeen he has been fascinated by the interaction between mindset and accomplishments. Tobias was inspired to write *Great Traits* after his close friend, a wounded soldier, became the first ever amputee to walk to the North Pole. All the author's proceeds from *Great Traits* are donated to the charity *Walking With The Wounded*. Aside from running the Great Traits Project, Tobias is an investor and researcher for a Wall Street financial firm. He has a degree from the University of Bath. *Great Traits* is his first book.

For speaking engagements please contact:
yes@greattraitsproject.com

To find out more about the behaviour and beliefs behind phenomenal feats visit GreatTraitsProject.com or @GreatTraitsPro or facebook.com/GreatTraitsProject

Nico Wills is a London based portrait, travel and wildlife photographer. Following a degree in Zoology from Edinburgh University he joined the army in 2009, commissioning into the Grenadier Guards. For the majority of 2012, he was deployed on Operations with the Grenadier Guards Battle Group in Afghanistan as a platoon commander in The Queen's Company. Nico carried his camera everywhere with him on his body armour to document the tour. In 2014, he held his first solo exhibition at Bonhams, raising money for the Regimental charity *The Colonel's Fund*. The exhibition, *Traces*, documented life in Afghanistan from a soldier's perspective. A year later his second exhibition, *Eye Contact*, focused on wildlife and the exhibition proceeds were donated to *The Cheetah Conservation Fund, The Colonel's Fund* and *The Household Cavalry Foundation*.

To see more of his work visit nicowills.com or contact: info@nicowills.com